D2

S/4 5020/9

Eat to Beat Indigestion

Eat to Beat Indigestion

The antacid action plan

Amanda Ursell

Thorsons
An Imprint of HarperCollins*Publishers*

The author would like to thank Warner Wellcome for the use of data from their NOP consumer survey on indigestion, in Chapter 5.

Thorsons
An Imprint of HarperCollins*Publishers*
77–85 Fulham Palace Road,
Hammersmith, London W6 8JB
1160 Battery Street,
San Francisco, California 94111–1213

Published by Thorsons 1996

1 3 5 7 9 10 8 6 4 2

© Amanda Ursell 1996

Amanda Ursell asserts the moral right to
be identified as the author of this work

A catalogue record for this book is available from the British Library

ISBN 0 7225 3253 9

Printed in Great Britain by
HarperCollinsManufacturing Glasgow

*For my parents – although this is
one book I hope you won't need to read!*

Contents

࿔

CHAPTER ONE

How Digestion Works

Indigestion – ask anyone to describe it and they'll all give a different answer. An acidy feeling in the stomach, an acidy feeling in the throat, bloated stomach, stomach pain, burning throat, heartburn, trapped wind, nausea, frequent belching and the list goes on.

It doesn't seem fair that two of life's great pleasures – eating and drinking – can lead to such uncomfortable side-effects. To get to the bottom of what causes it, you need to see how the digestive system operates when everything is working normally.

One of the trickiest ideas to grasp is that the system is, essentially, just one long tube surrounded by muscles that takes on different shapes and roles as it makes its way through the body. There are five main parts (see Figure 1).

The Five Sections of the Digestive Tract

All food and drink starts off in the mouth, where it is chewed and swallowed. Then they pass into the second part of the system, the gullet or oesophagus. The oesophagus runs down the throat, taking food and drink from the mouth into the third section, the stomach. The stomach is where the tube forms a pouch. After the stomach, it is a tube again and we are into the fourth section, the small intestine. The fifth and final section, the

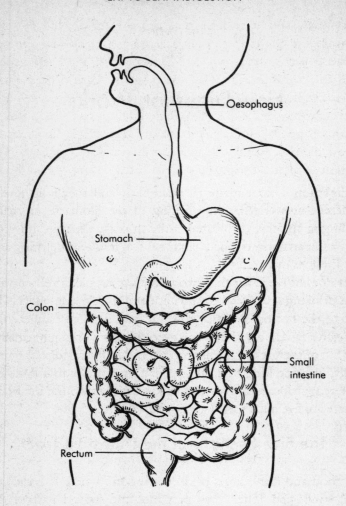

Figure 1 The digestive tract

large intestine, ends in the rectum and anus.

Each of these sections of the digestive tube has a different set of functions. These are controlled by a fine balance of nerves and hormones, and it is they that fire off signals for muscles surrounding the tract to contract and relax, and give the go-ahead for juices and enzymes to be secreted into it. Each section likes to do things at its own speed so that each process takes place not too quickly and not too slowly. The nerves and hormones have to be organized with military precision to ensure all this happens. Any signals that get out of step threaten to throw the process into chaos, with indigestion – at whichever section of the tract happens to be affected – being the unfortunate result.

The digestive system has one overriding function – to break down the nutrients in foods and drinks into the smallest forms possible so that they can be absorbed through the wall of the intestinal tract into the blood vessels surrounding it. The blood, in turn, can then transport the nutrients, carbohydrates, proteins, fats, vitamins and minerals around the body to cells and organs that need them to carry out life-maintaining jobs.

Take proteins. Proteins are found in meat, poultry, fish, eggs, cheese, nuts, seeds and beans. Proteins are big molecules made up from building blocks called amino acids. The body can not absorb whole proteins, so the job of the digestive tract is to break large proteins down into their constituents, the amino acids. It's rather like taking a house apart, brick by brick. Once the amino acids have been absorbed into the blood, they are carried around the body and are built back up into proteins – for example, in our muscles.

A similar process is involved when it comes to fats and carbohydrates. Fats are broken down into substances called fatty acids and glycerol before they can be absorbed. Carbohydrates occur in the diet in different sizes. Starches are the largest carbohydrate molecules, milk sugars and table sugar are smaller carbohydrates, and glucose, fructose and galactose are the smallest. The job of the digestive system is to break all these differently sized carbohydrates down into the smallest one – glucose, and only then can it be absorbed into the blood.

Think of it like a slot machine that can only take certain coins. The machine could not cope if you fed in any other coins – it can only take those particular ones. So, any other kinds of coins must first be changed into the required kind before they can be used. The same thing happens to food – it's broken down into the smallest denomination of each nutrient group before it is accept-able to and absorbed by the body.

The Mouth

The most enjoyable part of eating and drinking occurs in the mouth, where food and drink first enter the body. It's here that we experience the textures and flavours that register as being pleasurable in the brain.

As well as detecting the pleasurable aspects of food and drink, the mouth is the place where good digestion starts. Healthy teeth and gums play a vital role in the process, and tooth decay, gum disease and poorly fitted dentures are suprisingly common reasons for indigestion.

The mechanical action of physically chewing food is the first step in the digestive process. The teeth are of two kinds: incisors, which cut, and molars at the back of the mouth which grind the food we eat. The jaw muscles when working together can exert 91 kg (200 lbs) of pressure on the molars, so even tough meats and the most fibrous vegetables can begin to be broken down by them.

As well as breaking food down into pieces small enough to swallow, chewing mixes food with the mouth's secretion, saliva. As saliva contains fat and carbohydrate-breaking enzymes, food also starts undergoing its chemical breakdown in the mouth, too. Try chewing a piece of bread for a few minutes. As the salivary amylase enzymes start breaking the starchy carbohydrate in bread into simple sugars, the bread will begin to taste sweeter. The digestive enzymes only act on the *surfaces* of the foods they come into contact with. So, grinding the food into very small particles in the mouth – in other words, chewing food thoroughly – means that more enzymatic digestion can take place. It also eases the movement of the food down the gullet, through the stomach and into the next part of the intestine.

Saliva is important for several reasons. As well as containing the enzymes mentioned, it also has a physical role. That is to make the food moist, and therefore easier to swallow. You only have to try eating three or four cream crackers in a row without a drink to wash them down to know how hard it is to swallow once saliva starts drying up.

The secretion of saliva from salivary glands into the mouth is stimulated by the thought, sight and smell of food, and begins preparing the body for the food it's about to receive even before eating has started. It has another important role, too. The pH of saliva is on the alkaline side. This means it can help neutralize acidy foods and drinks as soon as they get into the mouth.

Once food has been chewed and mixed with saliva, it's time to swallow it. This is where the tongue springs into action. We swallow hundreds of times a day without giving a thought to how complicated this process is. In the way we learned during weaning, the tongue rises up and presses against the roof of the mouth. This forces the lump of food – or bolus as it's called in technical terms – into the back of the throat. This series of movements involves around 22 separate muscle groups. From here, rather like when you sit on a big dipper when the starter switch has been pressed, there's no going back. The bolus is swept into the back of the throat (called the pharynx), an action that stimulates muscles to contract and relax. This pulsating movement carries the bolus on into the oesophagus, or gullet as it's also known. From here it is carried, like a raft on the rapids, turbulently downwards to the stomach by wave-like contractions of muscles surrounding the oesophagus. The entire journey time from mouth to stomach is remarkably quick, taking a matter of four to eight seconds. Fluids travel even faster, whizzing through this part of the journey in one to two seconds.

To stop the bolus taking a wrong turning and shooting off into the windpipe instead of making its way on into the stomach, a small flap closes over the entrance to the windpipe to block it off. If you try to talk or inhale while swallowing, the protective mechanisms can be disrupted and shortcircuited, with food getting into the breathing passageways. If this happens, frantic coughing is triggered, which is the body's way of trying to expel the food as quickly as possible and stop you choking.

Throughout its meandering course through the body, the digestive system is punctuated by valves and 'gateways'. The first of these is situated just above the entrance to the stomach. Known as the lower oesophageal valve, it too is closed off until it detects the approach of the bolus making its way down the oesophagus. As the bolus gets close to the top of the stomach, the muscular valve, acting as a gateway, opens, allowing the lump of food to continue on, into the stomach, the bag-like storage tank of the digestive system.

The Stomach

The stomach is really a temporary reservoir. During the course of your life, it learns to accept a bewildering array of lumps of food and a wide variety of drinks. A bolus may be hard, soft, acidic, alkaline, watery or solid. Whatever form each bolus takes when it enters the stomach, by the time it's ready to go on into the small intestine it needs to have been turned from a solid into a liquid, and that liquid needs to be of a consistent pH – in other words, not too acidic and not too alkaline. To ensure this, the stomach carries out several functions.

Like the rest of the digestive tract, the stomach is surrounded by lots of muscles. It can vary in shape a little from one person to another, but is generally a 'J'-shaped bag (see Figure 2). In short, stout people, it tends to run horizontally, whereas in tall, thin people the J is more vertical.

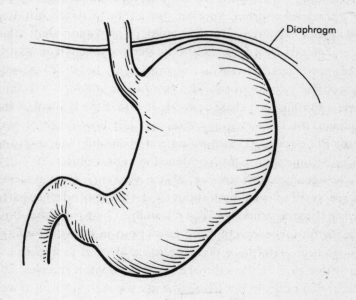

Figure 2 Diagram of the stomach, shaped like a 'J'-shaped bag

In either type of person, the stomach is surprisingly high up and not by the belly button, which is normally where we point to if complaining of stomach ache. When we are not eating (for example at night and about four hours after the last meal), the stomach is relatively empty and looks like a deflated balloon, about 25 cm (10 in) long. In this state, it holds about 50 ml (2 fl oz), one third of a small yogurt pot. Once full, however, it can really expand, holding up to 4 litres (7 pints) of food and drink. This comes in handy for feast days, highdays and holidays when we usually overindulge. After a normal meal, it would contain more like 1.5 to 2 litres (2½ to 3½ pints).

One of the stomach's main roles is to put the muscles surrounding it into action. By contracting and relaxing, they set up a powerful churning motion, like a cement mixer, grinding and mixing its contents. Just as a builder would add water to thin a cement mix down, so the body secretes mucus and gastric juices, produced in copious quantities in the stomach wall. Nerves and hormones take the role of the builder controlling these additions, but these in turn are under the control of the foreman, the brain, which judges carefully how much of each needs to be added. The churning continues and the mucus and juices become thoroughly combined with the bolus.

The signal to start secreting, as we have seen, is given as soon a we see, smell or even think about food – a sort of advance party, letting the stomach know it's on standby. Once food and drink actually hit the stomach, more juices pour in from the walls of the stomach – partly in response to its physical presence, and partly due to the chemical make-up of the bolus it receives. The mucus that pours in is alkaline. It coats the stomach wall as well as mixing with the food and softening it up.

The juices contain three substances:

- hydrochloric acid, which lowers the pH of the stomach environment and kills bugs

- pepsin, which is an enzyme that helps digest protein
- hormones, which control the contractions and movement of the muscular stomach.

The hydrochloric acid is extremely strong. When secreted, it immediately makes the stomach contents very acidic, with a pH of between 1.5 and 3.5 (neutral is pH 7). These acidic conditions are needed to help in the digestion of proteins and to kill off the many bacteria that enter the stomach in and with food and drink. Due to its low pH, hydrochloric acid is highly corrosive, apparently more so than the acid in a car battery, so that if the contents of the stomach were placed on a wooden table, they would bore their way through.

The acid clearly has a vital role, but the stomach wall has to be protected from it to avoid being damaged itself. Like most parts of the body when they are functioning properly, it has developed ways of getting round the potential problem. It does so in several ways. First, it has a thick coating of the alkaline mucus built up over it. Second, the cells of the stomach lining are very tightly cemented together, preventing gastric juices leaking into the tissues below. Third, if cells are damaged, they are quickly shed and replaced. The lining is completely shed and renewed every three to six days anyway to ensure that only fresh, protective cells are in place.

The nerves and hormones that control the secretions and movements communicate directly with the brain. The brain controls the movements and secretions by detecting the physical presence and chemical compostion of food in the stomach via the nerves and hormones. The brain also affects the stomach's movements in response to external stimuli. Any form of anxiety, stress, emotional turmoil, fright or depression will be detected in the brain and exert their effect, through the nerves, on the stomach. In times of intense stress, for example, it's unlikely that you will feel the need to eat and so you can lose your appetite. The link between how we feel and the effect this has on all parts of the digestive tract should never be underestimated.

Certain components and nutrients in food and drink that enter the stomach can also directly affect the secretion of mucus and juice, and the valves at the top and bottom of the stomach.

Alcohol, aspirin and water are virtually the only substances that are absorbed directly from the stomach into the blood-stream – the rest must pass on into the small intestine.

Over a period of a few hours, the bolus will have gradually been broken down into a liquidy substance known as chyme. This has to pass out of the stomach and on into the first section of the small intestine, called the duodenum.

The Small Intestine

After the stomach, the gut reverts to a tube shape, and this part of the digestive system is the small intestine. Only about 2.5 cm (1 in) wide, it's a staggering 2 m (2 yards) long. This great length of tubing is carefully arranged in the region we usually refer to as our stomach – the space below the ribcage. If the intestines were stretched out rather than being neatly folded as they are, we would be a very tall race.

The small intestine is where the bulk of the digestive process takes place. The stomach has mechanically turned the food and drink into the liquidy chyme described above, and between it and the mouth has already started chemically breaking down proteins, carbohydrates and fats. The small intestine, though, is sitting in wait with a complete army of enzymes to finish the job. It is here where proteins are broken down into their smallest form, amino acids, carbohydrates to simple sugars and fats to fatty acids and glycerol. It is here also where essential vitamins and minerals in foods are absorbed into the blood to be carried off to perform various functions around the body.

Under the microscope, the wall of the small intestine looks like grass blowing in the wind. This is because the wall is formed into very fine finger-like projections known as villi (see Figure 3). They are about a millimetre (less than ⅛ in) tall and feel velvety. Digested nutrients are absorbed through the wall of villi into little blood vessels which run inside them.

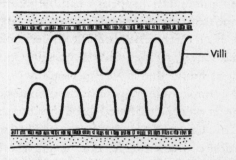

Figure 3 The villi on the walls of the small intestine.

The villi increase the absorbtive surface of the small intestine enormously – yet another space-saving device. It has been estimated that the entire absorptive surface these villi provide is equivalent to 200 sq. m (239 sq. yards). That is, the floor space of an average two-storey house. If there were no villi, the small intestine would have to be even longer than it already is.

Intestinal juices, which contain some of the necessary breakdown enzymes, are secreted from the walls of the intestine in quantities of 1 to 2 litres (1¾ to 3½ pints) a day. They pour into the intestine when the chyme leaves the stomach and enters the duodenum.

Enzymes are also secreted directly from the intestinal walls and from the pancreas – an organ that sits alongside the intestine and also secretes some enzymes. The pancreas is vital for another reason. The chyme from the stomach is still acidic at this point and must be made neutral so that it doesn't damage the intestine wall. The pancreas pumps alkaline juices into the intestine to effect this neutralization.

In addition to enzymes, the intestine receives a secretion from the gallbladder – another small organ situated close by. The gallbladder squirts in bile, which is a rather unpleasant-looking yellowy green liquid. This happens when the intestine registers that the chyme from the stomach is particularly fatty after a fat-rich meal has been eaten. The hormone cholecystokinin (CCK) acts as the messenger, racing from the intestine to tell the gallbladder to start firing. Bile is able to emulsify or homogenize fats. A good example of homogenization is homogenized milk, which has the fat evenly distributed throughout so that no cream line forms. This, essentially, is what bile does to fats in the intestine. It distributes them evenly, thus giving the fat-breaking enzymes a chance to get to work on them.

Food is moved down the tube by the muscles that surround it. They contract and relax rhythmically in a motion known as peristalsis (see Figure 4). These little waves of movement gradually push the contents forwards and backwards, offering them up to the villi to be absorbed.

The end of the small intestine is blocked off from the start of the final section of the system – the large intestine – by another valve. Nerves and hormones tell the valve to open to allow undigested material from the meal and bacteria to move on into the large intestine. The valve is important not so much for letting the material through, but for stopping contents of the large intestine creeping back into the small intestine.

The small intestine, like the stomach, is wired up to the brain

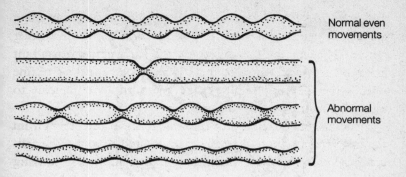

*Figure 4 Rhythmical movements – known as peristalsis –
in the small intestine push the contents along.*

via a huge number of nerves. Thus, any stress, anxiety or worries can again be transmitted to the system and affect its functioning in very significant ways.

The Large Intestine

This section is called 'large' because of its diameter rather than its length. It is 0.5 m (½ yard) shorter than the small intestine and considerably fatter. Its main function is to absorb water from indigestible food residues and to eliminate them from the body as semi-solid faeces (see Figure 5).

The large intestine is divided into sections:

- caecum
- appendix
- colon
- rectum
- anal canal.

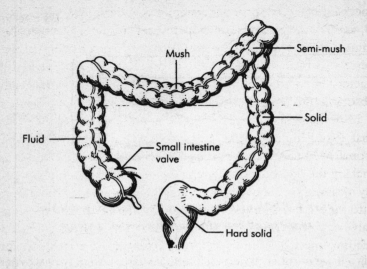

Figure 5 The semi-fluid contents of the small intestine are gradually turned into solids in the large intestine.

Most of the nutrients from food and drink have been absorbed once they reach the large intestine, so there is no reason to have all the little villi found on the surface of the small intestine. The surface is therefore flatter. No nutrient-breaking enzymes need to be secreted, but lots of mucus is secreted, which lubricates the passage of the faeces and protects the wall from irritating acids and gases formed by bacteria that live and beaver away in the large intestine.

The matter that reaches the large intestine will stay there for between 12 and 24 hours. It's being increasingly realized that the large intestine isn't just a storage system that allows waste to collect until you can reach a toilet. It does take part in the digestion of some remaining food residues (mostly carried out by specialist bacteria), produces vitamin K and the B vitamins B_{12}, B_1 and B_2, and allows water, sodium and chloride, plus the vitamins it's produced, to be absorbed into surrounding blood vessels. So-called short-chain fatty acids are produced by bacteria acting on fibre in this section of the gut and these are absorbed into the bloodstream.

Movement in the large intestine is nothing like as manic as that found higher up the digestive tract, in, for example, the stomach. In fact, it is like a rather lazy lizard basking in the sun, making the odd slow shuffling movement every half hour or so. By means of such movements, the residue is gradually shoved on into the rectum. Nerves tell the rectum to contract and the next valve or gate to open into the anal canal. Once faeces enter the rectum, messages are sent to the brain and we then decide whether the final valve of the whole system – the external anal valve – is to open and allow expulsion of faeces.

The large intestine is, like the rest of the gut, controlled by nerves that communicate with the brain and is affected by emotions and stress.

∾

CHAPTER TWO

Dyspepsia and Other Common Types of Indigestion

'Dys' is often used at the beginning of medical terms for symptoms and actually means 'difficult'. 'Pepsia' is the Greek word for 'cooked' or 'digested'. So 'dyspepsia', which is used to describe a wide range of symptoms – from butterflies in the stomach to pain below the breastbone, abdominal pain, bloating, belching and nausea – means 'difficult digestion'.

Digestion, as we saw in Chapter 1, involves food and drink passing from the mouth to the anus, with an awful lot of things going on between these points. It is hardly surprising, then, that any one of the huge range of activities taking place along the way can go wrong, get out of synch or simply break down.

Indigestion is often thought of as simply affecting the top part of the digestive tract, but in fact it can occur anywhere along the tract and be triggered by the types of food and drink eaten, the timing and way in which they are eaten, the nerves supplying the tract being affected by something, or any of the enzymes, hormones or other organs that supply the tract being adversely affected. The whole system is finely balanced and susceptible to many influences, which can throw it into disarray.

Straightforward dyspepsia – that is, when it does not have an underlying medical cause – is often experienced sporadically. It may be caused by certain foods or certain types of meals taken at a certain time of day. It can also be linked in with the brain-gut connection and therefore occur at stressful and emotionally draining times.

In the following chapters, the main problems that occur with digestion will be described and suggestions made as to how steps you can take in your diet and lifestyle can help avoid and overcome them. Before we get to this, though, let us start with the very beginning of digestion – when food and drink are consumed.

The Mouth

Good digestion starts in the mouth. It is essential to keep the teeth and gums in good condition to ensure that food can be chewed properly before it is swallowed. This means brushing our teeth twice daily and making regular trips to the dentist for check-ups. Problems with dentures, aches, mouth ulcers, cavities and infections can all affect both the types of food and drink consumed and how effectively the mouth can play its part in the digestive process. Poorly chewed food due, for example, to a decayed tooth because it hurts to chew with it, will start its journey in large lumps, which can cause discomfort in the throat and take longer to digest further down the tract as it has not been broken up sufficiently.

To help avoid decay, don't eat sugary foods and drinks between meals and either brush your teeth after eating or chew a gum containing xylitol, which helps bring the acid levels in the mouth back to normal and therefore prevents decay.

Dysphagia (Problems with Swallowing)

The only role the oesophagus has is that of transferring food from the mouth to the stomach. Most problems with this part of the 'tube' therefore lead to some kind of problem with swallowing, which is called dysphagia. If swallowing is affected then, invariably, this has far-reaching effects on nutrient intake as it, more often than not, leads to a reduction in food consumption.

Painful swallowing may be caused by a variety of problems, including infections such as the flu or tonsillitis. These need to be treated by your doctor.

Problems with the muscles and nerves that supply the oesophagus and trigger the waves of contraction and relaxation that push food down into the stomach can lead to dysphagia, too. Parkinson's disease will cause this kind of problem and should again, obviously, be treated by the doctor.

A goitre occurs when the thyroid gland (situated in the throat) swells, which often leads to difficulties with swallowing, too, this time because the goitre presses on the tract, restricting its width. Again, this is a problem your doctor will need to treat.

Inflammation of the oesophagus, due to regurgitation or refluxing of acidic stomach contents, can lead to ulceration and, if it continues, narrowing of the tract. In children it is possible for such problems of inflammation to arise from swallowing substances like bleach or caustic soda.

In people with a depleted immune system, candidiasis can lead to swallowing difficulties, too.

If you become anaemic as a result of a lack of iron in your diet, it is possible that the lining of the mouth, back of the throat and oesophagus will break down. Liquids can be taken, but eating solid foods can be painful. This is treatable by taking iron supplements to cure the anaemia.

In addition to all these causes of swallowing difficulties, there are simpler ones, too. Stress can affect this part of the tract, as it can other sections. Here, it can speed up contractions, making swallowing uncomfortable.

The sensation of having a lump in the throat can also, in some cases, be put down to psychological factors. This can be triggered by emotion – most of us will have experienced feeling 'choked up' at some time or another. In some people, this feeling persists once the immediate source of emotion has passed. Crying can sometimes relieve the feeling, as can eating and drinking. Treating the cause of the emotional distress is often the best course of action in such circumstances.

If you have these sensations and there are no underlying medical reasons, then it is time to think about diet and lifestyle and the ways in which you eat. This is because what you eat may have an effect on swallowing. It has been shown, for example, that gulping down a very cold drink can bring about a short-lived paralysis, which temporarily blocks the progress of food and causes chest pain.

The wide range of potential causes of digestive problems associated with the throat means that it is vital that any difficulties with swallowing be checked out by your doctor.

Dietary Advice

Once your doctor has identified the problem, advice on what to eat to keep nutrient intakes up is important. If swallowing needs to be relearned, then the help of both a speech therapist and a dietitian is invaluable.

Generally, the best foods to try if swallowing is a problem are those that are soft, need little chewing and will slip down easily. Chilled soft foods, like ice-cream, jellies, smooth yogurt, fromage frais, mousses and thick custard are good starting points. Slightly chilled foods are good, too, because they stimulate the swallowing reflex more easily than do warm ones. This is because there are more receptors that register cold temperatures at the back of the mouth than there are that register warm ones.

As swallowing improves, then you can move on to mixed consistency foods.

Heartburn

Heartburn is one of the commonest forms of indigestion, and the one people are usually describing when they complain of an 'acidy' taste in the throat and/or mouth. Heartburn occurs when the acid contents of the stomach spill back, past the sphincter into the gullet or oesophagus. On occasions, they may actually reflux right the way back and up into the mouth.

It's important to get the idea of reflux into perspective. Small amounts of reflux are actually perfectly normal and happen to most of us, most of the time. The muscular valve or gateway to the stomach allows some of the acidic mix of half-digested food to leak back out. It is in particularly susceptible people and those in whom large quantities seep out that the problem is both painful in the short term and a potential problem in the long term.

When you stop and think about it, it's hardly surprising that heartburn hurts. The stomach, as we saw in Chapter 1, is equipped to deal with the acidic nature of its contents by having a thick, duvet-like coating of mucus to protect its surface. The oesophagus has no such protection. Swallowing saliva, which is alkaline, can help to neutralize the normal, small amounts of regurgitated acidic material, and the swallowing action itself helps to sweep these stomach contents back down to where they belong. If any is left, however, or reflux gets out of hand, the acid can literally start digesting the surface cells of the gullet and back of the throat. This is what causes the nerves to register pain.

Heartburn is most likely to occur when the valves at the top of the stomach and bottom of the gullet become weakened (see

Figure 6). This is common in pregnancy when, it is believed, the extra levels of the hormone progesterone that are circulating have this weakening effect. Smoking is also thought to loosen the sphincter, as are certain drugs.

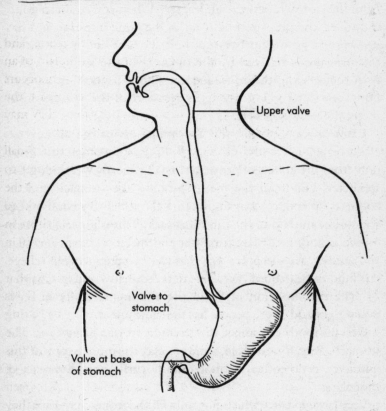

Figure 6 The valves of the gullet and stomach.

In other cases, the sphincter may be perfectly fit, but the pressure of, say, bending or lying down or lifting something heavy can overcome its ability to hold the stomach contents in and so

21

leakage follows. Lying down soon after eating can lead to acid reflux, too. The stomach is physically tipped up and some of its contents forced past the valve and into the gullet.

Constipation, perhaps rather surprisingly, can cause reflux from the stomach into the gullet, too. When you strain to go to the toilet, the pressure builds up in the large intestine and has nowhere to go except back up the tract. The end result is that this pressure is relieved by the opening of the stomach valve, with reflux being the consequence. This is a good example of how something going wrong in one part of the gut can indirectly affect another part.

Extra pressure within the abdominal cavity has an adverse effect on sphincter strength as well. Pregnant women suffer not only from the effects of progesterone chemically weakening the sphincter, but from the foetus pushing the stomach and its contents up and, once again, forcing the stomach's contents up and out of the top of the intestinal sack. This is especially likely to occur during the last trimester and making changes to diet and lifestyle are the only steps that can be taken to help relieve this kind of heartburn (these are detailed below and in Chapter 7). The accumulation of fat in the abdominal cavity in both overweight and obese people has the same effect.

Certain foods can affect the strength of this gateway to the stomach. Fats, for example, seem to relax the muscle tone of the sphincter, as do coffee, alcohol, onions, garlic, peppermints and chocolates.

Very large meals – which not only fill the stomach to capacity, but also sit around for hours and take ages to digest – will often lead to reflux. This is usually an infrequent cause of problems, occurring at, say, Christmas, special parties and dinners and so on, and so shouldn't be unduly worried over. It is just nature's way of letting you know you've overdone it.

Heartburn is made worse in susceptible people by severe emotional upset. The brain-gut connection reacts, with fear, anxiety and anger stimulating reflux.

Above the stomach, there sits a big band of muscle separating the stomach from the lungs. Called the diaphragm, it is possible for the top part of the stomach to push up and through this muscular barrier, creating a hiatus hernia (see Figure 7). Quite a few sufferers experience reflux and heartburn as a result of having a hernia.

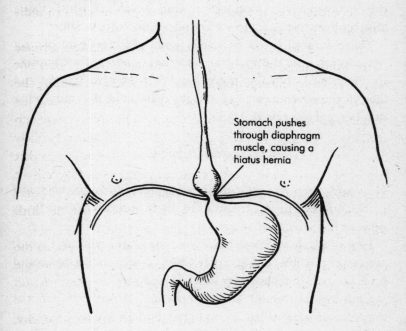

Stomach pushes through diaphragm muscle, causing a hiatus hernia

Figure 7 How a hiatus hernia is formed.

In a few people, the refluxing of the stomach's contents into the gullet can lead to inflammation. Severe cases may result in bleeding, which, if it carries on over a period of time, can lead to anaemia. The inflammation, or oesophagitis as it's known, may eventually cause scarring and a narrowing of the gullet. This is obviously uncomfortable and may ultimately lead to cancer.

As you can see, it is vital that any serious refluxing is reported to your doctor, who may decide to investigate and look into things further. An investigation with an endoscope might be recommended, which involves swallowing a narrow tube – the endoscope – which has a camera and light in the end to enable the doctor to have a good look around and also take little tissue samples from the gullet to study under a microscope later.

There is a plethora of drugs and remedies available on prescription from the doctor or over the counter at the chemist's for heartburn. Equally, there are many positive dietary and lifestyle improvements you can make that can help to reduce the number and severity of attacks.

Dietary Advice

How and when you eat cannot be separated from the chemical composition of the food and drink itself in terms of the effects on your digestive system.

First of all, always try to make time to eat and drink and avoid, whenever possible, doing either when on the go. Sit down and leave yourself time, however short of it you are.

Chewing thoroughly is also important. It not only gets the digestive process off to a good start by thoroughly mixing in enzymes and turning food into small and easy-to-swallow pieces, it helps avoid the 'bolting' down of a meal or snack.

If you make yourself calm prior to eating and take the whole process at a more leisurely pace, your nervous system will calm down and produce less acid in the stomach.

Timings and Quantities

It's best to avoid huge influxes of food and drink at any one time to reduce the risk of overfilling the stomach. The stomach holds 1.5 litres (2½ pints) comfortably without becoming badly overextended. If too much is eaten at one go, the stomach becomes overfull, it cannot empty itself fast enough to clear it and reflux is likely.

This means it's important not to skip meals, only to overindulge several hours later. Small, regular intakes – such as a light breakfast, mid morning snack, lunch, mid-afternoon snack and finally a light evening meal – is the best pattern to adopt to avoid reflux and heartburn. It is vital that you leave time after your last meal of the day for the food to start moving from the stomach into the intestine – in other words, a good few hours before going to bed. The risk of *not* following such a rule is that, as soon as you lie down, the contents of the stomach move into the oesophagus by sheer virtue of gravity. So, why deliberately make things worse for yourself?

The Chemical Composition of Foods

Certain components of foods and drinks can actually weaken the sphincter at the top of the stomach.

Protein-rich meals seem to enhance the tone of the valve, making it tighter and, therefore, a better blocker. Good sources of protein include lean meat, poultry without the skin, fish (white and oily), eggs and reduced-fat dairy products, such as milk and cheese.

Fatty foods have quite the opposite effect. Meals and snacks rich in fat *relax* the sphincter, making reflux and therefore heartburn in susceptible people more likely. Most people in the West consume more calories than necessary from fats and would be well advised to reduce their totals for other health reasons. Diets rich in fat are more likely to lead to putting on weight. If high in saturated fatty acids, they can increase cholesterol levels in the blood and thus the risk of heart disease.

Fats have another action on the stomach that can make heartburn more likely. When a fat-rich bolus reaches the stomach, small bits of it are passed on into the top part of the small intestine. In this section, the duodenum, it is recognized that the fat content is high, which stimulates the release of a hormone called enterogastrin. This hormone acts as a messenger and tells the muscles of the stomach to slow down its contractions. With the movements of the muscles reduced, the mixing and grinding takes longer and food stays in the stomach for greater periods of time. In those who suffer refluxes, the time period over which it could occur is therefore increased as a fatty meal can remain in the stomach for up to four or five hours.

Cutting back on fat is important from a weight point of view, too. As mentioned, fatty diets tend to lead to weight gain. Gram for gram, fats contain twice the calories of carbohydrates and protein, so a teaspoon of fat such as butter, margarine or oil will provide 37 calories while a teaspoon of a protein food like lean beef will provide around 10. A fatty diet is therefore far more energy dense than one rich in carbohydrates and proteins. That is, many more calories are packed into a small quantitiy of fatty foods than are contained in carbohydrates and proteins.

It's easy to moniter the amount of fats we take in when we can actually *see* them. These so-called 'visible fats' are things like butter, margarines and oils. They are all virtually 100 per cent pure fat and are very high in calories. Much more of a problem are the fats lurking in foods, and in some cases drinks, that are well disguised. Looking on the packets of foods often gives the game away. If fats, oils, margarine or butter appear high up on the list of ingredients, then it is sure to contain a fair amount of them as ingredients are listed in order of the quantity used, with whatever there is most of appearing first and whatever there is least of appearing last. There are many foods containing such hidden fats that, in theory, aren't a surprise. Biscuits and cakes, creamy foods and things that are fried are bound to be rich in fats. Sometimes the actual quantities they contain can be quite staggering though. (Note that the imperial conversions below are rounded up or down and so are the approximate equivalents of the grams figures.)

Hidden Fats in Foods

2 shortbread fingers	9 g (⅓ oz)
2 coconut cookies	5 g (⅕ oz)
2 lemon puffs	10 g (⅓ oz)
Original crunchy bar	7 g (¼ oz)
Cherry bakewell	7 g (¼ oz)
Apple pie	8 g (¼ oz)
Puff slice	12 g (½ oz)
Flapjack slice	6 g (⅕ oz)
Viennese whirl	13 g (½ oz)
Cheese and tomato pizza (200g)	20 g (¾ oz)
Pork pie	37 g (1⅓ oz)
Steak and kidney pie	22 g (¾ oz)
2 pork sausages	30 g (1 oz)
Cornish pasty	29 g (1 oz)
Sausage roll	16 g (½ oz)
Fish and chips	38 g (1⅓ oz)
Coleslaw (per 50 g/2 oz)	8 g (¼ oz)

Savoury snacks are an area to really watch. Most are based on potatoes or corn and are then fried. Both potato and corn are able to absorb large amounts of fats during frying so will be literally dripping in calories.

Snack	Packet Size	Calories	Fat
Bombay mix	100 g (4 oz)	494	32 g (1 oz)
Potato crisps	30 g (1 oz)	160	11 g (⅓ oz)
Peanuts	25 g (1 oz)	143	12 g (½ oz)
Trail mix	100 g (4 oz)	495	31 g (1 oz)
Les mignons	100 g (4 oz)	515	35 g (1¼ oz)
Tortilla chips	100 g (4 oz)	490	25 g (1 oz)

Other foods to be aware of are those with added cheese. Cheese is an excellent source of protein and calcium. However, it is also high in fats, the amount varying depending on the type, so if cheese is sprinkled over something such as a pizza or jacket potato, the totals of fat and calories will shoot up.

Returning to the valve. This little muscular ring at the entrance to the stomach is suseptible to chemicals in food over and above just proteins and fats. Perhaps one of the most surprising of these is peppermint. It is fairly traditional to serve mints after a meal as they do aid digestion further down the tract. In those who are prone to gastric reflux, the best advice is to pass on them. The peppermint acts as a smooth muscle relaxant. When it comes into contact with the sphincter, therefore, it will cause it to relax and lose tone, making it easier for the stomach contents to leak back into the oesophagus.

Caffeine, found in coffee, tea and cola, has a similar effect, making the ritual of coffee and mints after a meal a complete nightmare for the refluxer. The amount of caffeine commonly found in just one or two cups of coffee has been shown to slightly relax the valve just 30 to 45 minutes after drinking it.

If the mints are coated in chocolate, this will truly seal your fate as chocolate is yet another substance that will relax the valve acting as the stomach's gatekeeper. The effect of chocolate on the valve may be due to its methylxanthine content. Methylxanthines are related to the caffeine family of substances. Drinking hot chocolate, even the reduced fat versions, before going to bed is also a habit best discouraged if heartburn is a problem.

Alcohol weakens the muscular valve, too, so, again, go easy, and a liqueur is the last the thing you need after a big meal.

Some evidence suggests that onions and garlic have adverse effects on valve tone, too, so it is worth testing the theory out and seeing if reducing them in the diet works for you.

Concentrated solutions of sugar or salt may directly irritate the oesophageal membranes that have already been damaged by reflux. This may explain why some fruit juices and tomato juice are poorly tolerated. The high sugar concentration may be more irritating than the acid content. Spicy foods can also have a direct, negative effect on the already damaged areas.

Action Plan

Heartburn due to reflux is painful and distressing and eventually will take the enjoyment out of eating and drinking. Reduce the risks of reflux by following the simple rules below.

Plan Your Meals

Make time for your meals, however little spare you have, by setting aside a calm 20 minutes to eat and drink. Eating on the hoof can be a false economy where time is concerned if following the meal you are then debilitated by uncomfortable refluxing.

One way of slowing down is to use a different method of eating to the one you normally use. Try chopsticks, for example. If you are not practised in using them, they will definitely slow you down, although, of course, this isn't very practical when you are out in restaurants or with friends.

Chew slowly. Start by training yourself to chew everything 40 times before swallowing. It has a remarkably calming effect and presents food to your stomach in a more digestible form.

Eat little and often. Plan your day so that you don't have any heavy meals at night time. If you get peckish in the evenings, then stick to light fruits or yogurts. The diet plan given in Chapter 7 has been designed to enable you to do this.

Avoid cigarette smoking, especially in the evening before going to bed, as this weakens the valve to the stomach.

Get the overall balance of your diet right by including the correct amounts of starchy carbohydrates, proteins, fats and sugars. Again, the plan in Chapter 7 sets these out, with about 50 per cent of the total calories coming from carbohydrates, 15 per cent from proteins and 35 per cent from fats. It also contains at least five servings of fruit and vegetables a day.

Drinks

As a rule, try to avoid coffee and strong tea, as well as hot chocolate and cola drinks. Decaffeinated versions of tea, coffee and cola can be found, but, still, go easy as they do contain some caffeine.

Alternatives include drinks such as Barley Cup and Caro, herb teas and herb-based soft drinks, such as Purdys and Aqua Libra, and you can't go wrong with straightforward still water.

Intakes of alcohol do need to be controlled and kept to a minimum because, as we have seen, it is able to loosen the stomach valve.

The Antiheartburn Diet given in Chapter 7 takes into account all of the factors mentioned and includes three light meals with snacks in between. The diet is high in fibre, low in fat, has plenty of carbohydrates and avoids onions, garlic, caffeine, alcohol, chocolate and fruit juices.

Gastritis

Gastritis means inflammation of the stomach, or gastric, lining. It is one form of dyspepsia and occurs when the top layers of cells in the stomach lining actually allow the acidic contents through. This immediately sets up inflammation, causing anything from mild discomfort to severe and repeated vomiting. When it is not related to a serious disease, a sudden, short, sharp burst of gastritis can be caused by something as simple as an alcoholic binge at a party. This erodes a small part of the stomach lining, letting the acid leak through to underlying areas. Mild to moderate gastritis is exceedingly common, but especially as we grow older.

Gastritis can also be triggered by the excess production of hydrochloric acid, which damages the gastric mucous membranes. Caffeine, for example, is capable of stimulating such hydrochloric acid production, causing localized damage. The patch is quickly repaired and symptoms usually pass in a couple of days.

Drugs such as aspirin have a similar effect, as can ingestion of plant or bacterial toxins in foods.

Gastritis that lasts for more than just a few days is more of a problem. Seek medical advice to determine the reasons behind it. Again dietary and lifestyle pointers are useful here and these include advice such as to avoid alcohol, eat small, regular meals, don't smoke or expose yourself to others' smoke and get plenty of rest.

Dietary Advice

It is important to cut out all the potential irritants in the diet to avoid inflaming the cells of the stomach lining. The odd alcoholic binge is not as worrying as a high constant intake. Limit alcohol intake to the safe limits, which are less than 14 units a week for women and less than 21 for men (a unit is, and these are standard pub measures, ½ pint of beer, 1 glass of wine, 1 measure of spirits or 1 glass of sherry). It is best to spread this intake throughout the week rather than have it in just a couple of goes. This is true for both men and women, and not only to help prevent alcohol-induced gastritis, but also to save the liver from the damaging effects of large onslaughts of alcohol, too.

Also, try to limit your caffeine intake and think carefully about when you do drink coffee, tea or colas. Powdered cold remedies usually contain quite large amounts of caffeine, so check the labels and avoid taking them if you can. The most damage is done when these drinks are taken on an otherwise empty stomach as there is then no other food or drink to dilute them. You will recall that caffeine stimulates the production of hydrocholoric acid by the cells in the stomach wall. If acid production increases but there is no food to mix it in with, it can irritate the walls of the stomach, leading to gastritis.

The Caffeine Contents of Drinks per 150 ml (¼ pint)

Filter coffee	100 mg
Instant coffee	70 mg
Tea	40 mg
Cola	18 mg
Drinking chocolate	3 mg
Decaffeinated coffee	3 mg
Decaffeinated tea	3 mg

Other sources of caffeine include dark chocolate, which has 40 mg in a 50g (2oz) piece, milk chocolate, which contains 10 mg for the same size piece and a cold remedy, which can have about 50 mg per sachet.

Spices contain volatile oils, which are also capable of physically irritating the stomach lining. This is a purely direct physical reaction, unlike the chain of events set in motion by caffeine production. Hot curries, chillies and chilli sauces used in Mexican and other foods and some drinks, like spicy tomato juices, Virgin and Bloody Marys are best avoided. A very hot chilli or curry dish that contains a blend of pungent spices can literally bore a hole in the stomach lining.

Foods to Eat
- Dairy products, such as milk, milky drinks, yogurts, fromage frais, cottage cheese, custards and rice puddings.
- Foods rich in soluble fibre, which includes porridge oats and stewed apples and pears.
- Soft, non-acidic fruits, including melons, guavas, papayas and apricots – both dried and rehydrated.
- Root vegetables, including potatoes, turnips and parsnips.

Foods to Avoid
- Spicy dishes, such as curries, if you are not used to them.
- Chillies in dishes and drinks. As above.

Drinks to Take
- Skimmed milk-based drinks, using coffee and tea substitutes.
- Vegetable juices not based on tomato, such as carrot.
- Water.

Drinks to Avoid
- Fruit juices.
- Tomato juice.
- Coffee.

- Tea.
- Cola drinks.

Bloating

Bloating may be due to a food intolerance. Common intolerances that lead to bloating include an inability to deal with the milk sugar, lactose (for further details, see Chapter 3).

Bloating can, however, be explained as being an occasional reaction to a certain type of food, such as cabbage or swede, or the result of an excessive amount of wind accumulating in the intestine. A sudden influx of high-fibre foods, especially pulses, can have this effect, too, while swallowing too much air is another cause. This last explanation may sound rather strange, but we all swallow air every time we speak, eat and drink. Eating in a rush, having large quantities of foods containing air, such as soufflés and meringues, and gulping down lots of carbonated drinks, all these things encourage extra air to be swallowed. However, this is easily remedied.

Dietary Advice

Again, the way in which you approach eating and drinking affects your digestion. Taking time and sitting down are essential. Chewing thoroughly and taking the whole process slowly will help reduce the amount of air swallowed with food. Gulping down foods and drinks will mean that you are taking in quite large quantities of air with each mouthful. Talking while eating has a similar effect, as does eating with your mouth open.

Avoid carbonated drinks. These introduce more unwanted air. Use plain water and still juices rather than fizzy water and orange, lemon, cola and other such drinks. It helps, too, to drink from a glass rather than straight from a bottle or can.

Chewing gum also causes you to swallow extra air. If you are having problems with excess wind, then try avoiding gum for a while to see if things improve at all.

When increasing the fibre content of your diet, remember to do so gradually. Start by making small, single changes, for example, just swapping from white to wholemeal bread. Gradually progress to including extra fruit and vegetables and, finally, start increasing the amounts of pulses, like beans and peas, in your diet. This allows the intestine time to get used to these foods and to produce the correct bacteria in the large intestine to deal with them, which will help keep the problem of bloating – which often accompanies a switch to a high-fibre diet – under control.

If bloating is a symptom of irritable bowel syndrome (IBS), see the section on this later in this chapter.

Burping and Belching

Burping and belching, like clothes and food, are subject to fashions and trends. Considered a sign of appreciation after a good meal back in Tudor times, burping after a dinner party nowadays would offend and embarrass the other people there. So, burping and belching are now largely consigned unceremoniously to the indigestion category as something we want to avoid.

Both long, hearty belches and short, sharp burps are, whatever your attitude towards them, a perfectly normal part of the digestive process, as they help to expel air that has collected in the stomach. While a baby is growing in the womb, the digestive tract is free from air. Once born, from the first inhalation of breath, the system gradually takes in air, especially when feeding, making it inevitable that the baby will need to burp.

When we need to burp, this indicates that quite a bit of air has accumulated in the stomach. This can produce symptoms varying from mild discomfort to quite unbearable cramping pain. Releasing the air from the stomach, up into the oesophagus and out of the mouth gives almost immediate relief.

Once again, eating habits, smoking and lifestyle all affect the quantity of air swallowed and produced. If air were water, straightforward swallowing involves taking down about a teaspoonful. Eating quickly, chatting, laughing, smoking and consuming carbonated drinks all increase the quantity of air swallowed and the necessity to bring it back up as burps or belches.

Dietary Advice

The advice for belching is very similar to that for bloating. It is especially important in this case to eat slowly and not to eat and talk at the same time as this encourages large amounts of air to be swallowed along with the food.

Chewing gum is also not recommended, and, as advised for bloating, avoid carbonated drinks.

Eat and drink slowly, making time for both. Doing either quickly will lead to swallowing large amounts of air and so aggravate belching problems.

An infusion of ginger can help relieve the need to belch. Try pouring boiling water into a cup containing a teaspoon of freshly grated ginger root and leave the mixture to stand for five minutes before straining off the liquid and drinking it. Alternatively, you could try chewing a ginger biscuit.

If you don't suffer from reflux, sucking a strong peppermint may also help relieve the problem.

Gently rubbing the stomach can help dislodge any trapped wind in the stomach, as can bending down from the waist or taking gentle exercise.

Food Diaries

If you suffer regularly from bloating and belching, and, indeed, flatulence (covered later in this chapter), dietary culprits can often be identified by keeping a food diary. This involves writing down everything you eat and drink over a five or seven-day period. It is necessary to record the times the food and drink were consumed and how you felt at the meal – whether it was rushed, whether you sat and had it quietly and so on. You also then need to record the time and severity of any symptoms that follow.

Over the course of a week, it should be possible to identify whether certain foods, drinks or situations are regularly precipitating the problem. It may seem like a chore, but this is a proven method of identifying causes of problems. For instance, a lot of people who suffer migraines complete such diaries to help identify trigger factors for their severe and debilitating headaches.

You can create your own food diary by buying a small notebook or just stapling a few sheets of paper together and creating a table set out like the following example.

Looking at this food diary, the information indicates that breakfast is not a problem. By mid-afternoon, however, the effect of lunch is showing up as a gassy, bloated feeling. This could have been due to rushing the food down and having a fizzy cola drink. If there were lots of beans in the chilli and it was very hot and spicy, this could have led to the bloating.

Food Diary
Date:

Food/ drink	Amount	Time	Type of meal	Time taken to consume	Feelings	Symptoms
Toast	x 2	8 am	Small	10 mins	Rushed	None
Butter	1 tsp					
Jam	1 tsp					
Tea	cup					
Baked potato	x1	1 pm	Medium	15 mins	Rushed	None
Chilli sauce						
Cola	Glass					
Tea						
Bun	x1	3 pm	Snack	5 mins	Rushed	Gassy, bloated
Meat	Small	8 pm	Dinner	30 mins	Quiet	OK
Cabbage	2 tbsp					
Carrots	2 tbsp					
Potatoes	x 3					
Treacle tart	1 slice					
Cream	Dollop					
Coffee						
Tea	Cup	10 pm	10 mins		Quiet	Belching, full

The snack in the afternoon didn't cause problems, but dinner looks quite heavy and, later in the evening, resulted in a full feeling and belching. The cabbage may have caused the belching and the fatty, heavy dessert led to that uncomfortable fullness, which is a bad state to go to bed in.

It may have been better to have had a fish or low-fat cheese filling with the baked potato at lunchtime and a still drink instead of a fizzy one and to have left more time to eat it, too. For dinner, substituting a different green vegetable, such as spinach or broccoli, and following this with a lighter dessert, like baked apple with fromage frais, may have helped avoid the problem.

Flatulence

With belching, excess air in the intestinal tract comes up and out of the mouth and is usually air that has previously been swallowed. With flatulence, the excess air is expelled from the other end of the tract and has usually been produced in the large intestine itself. Flatulence can be embarrassing and uncomfortable, but there are times when diet can play a role in relieving symptoms.

Flatus is comprised of over 250 different gases. The tendency to produce a lot of wind runs in families, as does the quantity of particular gases in it. Women tend to produce more of certain gases, such as methane, than men, and the amount increases as people get older.

Nitrogen, a little oxygen, hydrogen, carbon dioxide and methane are the main gases in wind, making up 99 per cent of those present. Hydrogen is made in the large intestine by bacteria, which feed on certain carbohydrates in the diet that cannot be broken down and absorbed in the normal way in the small intestine higher up. So, instead of being digested and absorbed, they carry on into the large intestine and become an energy source for the bacteria.

Hydrogen can be produced by bacteria feasting on two sugars found in beans, which are not digested by our systems further up. They also produce carbon dioxide and methane. Baked beans are notorious for creating wind and this is why they do so. It is possible that the gut adapts to the beans the more of them you eat, which would explain why this effect seems to lessen when beans are a regular feature in the diet over long periods, and why people who naturally include large amounts in their diets do not experience such problems.

It has been observed that people either produce methane or they don't, the former being the majority. In America, it has been proven that those of Oriental and Indian origin produce less methane than blacks and Caucasians. Why this is so is not really known, although it could be related to diet.

It has also been found that some antibiotics could change methane-producing phenomena, as can colonic irrigation.

It is the remaining 1 per cent of gases that tend to be those which give wind its noxious smells. Sulfide, for example, smells of rotten eggs, and ammonia is not too pleasant either.

Dietary Advice

A high-fibre diet that includes lots of fruits and vegetables along with wholegrain cereals, seeds and nuts is generally advocated in the promotion of good health. Increasing your intake of such foods suddenly, though, will undoubtedly increase the amount of gas produced. If you are unused to larger quantities of them, therefore, it may be best to include more of these foods gradually until the system adapts.

There are certain foods that seem to almost universally give people wind. These include Jerusalem artichokes, which contain a carbohydrate called inulin that cannot be digested, onions and green peppers, which provide the bacteria in the gut with food and have sulphur-containing compounds, and, of course, beans, with the carbohydrates stacchyose and raffinose, which also provide gut bacteria with food. Peas, also from the legume family, swede, Brussels sprouts and spinach can also create problems. Try your own little experiment. If you usually have problems after a Sunday lunch that includes swede, leave it out the next week and replace it with another vegetable to see if the problems decrease.

If wind is a real problem, then consult your doctor. It is possible for your GP, in conjunction with a state registered dietitian (SRD), to put you on to an exclusion diet to pinpoint the real offenders. They can then help you rebuild an eating plan that keeps the situation under control, but means you are still eating healthily.

Nausea

When there is no clear reason for feeling queasy and your doctor has ruled out any serious disease being the cause, yet waves of nausea keep occurring, it could be that the normal movements in the stomach are being disturbed. These movements are controlled by nerves and hormones, which can become unsynchronized. When this happens, the movements may speed up, slow down or get generally out of step with each other, throwing the stomach into disarray and creating that sick feeling, even when you haven't been overindulging in rich goodies or alcohol.

Stress may contribute to the chaotic muscular motions, and check with your doctor if any drugs you take may have this effect.

Dietary Advice

Nausea can be relieved by nibbling dry biscuits or toast and sipping water.

If the nausea has been stimulated by a food aversion, when the thought, smell or sight of a certain dish makes you feel ill, try to think of something else or move away from the offending dish. Psychological food aversions can often lead to feelings of nausea and are hard to overcome as they are usually deep-rooted.

Food aversions often date back to childhood. Most adults can recall something from the school dinner menu that literally makes them feel sick at the very thought of it. Semolina, over-cooked cabbage, processed peas, lumpy custard and warm milk are some of those most commonly mentioned.

Foods used as a medicine have been known to trigger aversions, too. Before the days of suntan cream, some ex-pats living in hot countries would rub vinegar into their children's skin in the hope it would stop them burning. This often led to the development of a lifelong aversion to vinegar, so these children when they grew up could not eat anything containing it, from mayonnaise to vinegar on chips.

Aversions to a particular food may be related to a time of trauma. Perhaps foods being eaten at the moment of receiving bad news or during a particularly bad family argument will be forever associated with that incident and bring on feelings of nausea if they are eaten in the future. The causes are numerous and individual and should never be lightly dismissed.

If the aversion is truly psychological, the food or drink that causes the sweeping feelings of nausea can be given in a disguised form and will not cause any problems. It is the mental picture created when the item is in full view that stirs the memories and sets the waves of nausea off. It is best to accept that you have such an aversion and avoid the foods that cause the problems.

If you are overcome by general nausea, restrict foods that have a strong smell and are highly flavoured as these can make the feeling worse. Any woman who has been pregnant and suffered from morning sickness will know the ones that cause problems. Cooked cabbage, percolated coffee, curries and heated oils for frying have strong smells that linger and often cause nausea. Highly flavoured dishes, again, like curry, and dishes using lots of garlic and pepper should also be avoided.

As a rule, avoid fatty and oily foods, too. This includes anything fried, as well as pastry, in the form of pasties, sausage rolls, tarts and desserts. Keep butter and margarines to a minimum at such times and try to have bread and toast without either. Savoury snacks are usually packed with fats, and these include all crisps, tortilla chips, nuts and seeds.

If nausea is brought on by overindulging in rich foods and alcohol, avoid both for several days, preferably longer, and think back to how bad you felt next time you are tempted to overindulge again.

Foods that are usually well tolerated when you are feeling nauseous include vegetable soups, steamed vegetables and plain carbohydrates, such as rice, bread, boiled potatoes, buckwheat and couscous.

Snacks that can often be tolerated and may even alleviate nausea include:

- breakfast cereals with skimmed milk
- toast with jam but no butter or margarine
- plain biscuits, e.g. Marie, Arrowroot and Rich Tea
- hot or cold skimmed milk drinks
- boiled egg with toast but with no butter or margarine
- baked beans on toast but with no butter or margarine

- vegetable soup and toast with no butter or margarine
- jacket potato with low-fat yogurt
- low-fat milk pudding
- low-fat custard
- fruit salad with low-fat yogurt.

Gastric Ulcers

Ulcers can occur in the stomach, which account for about 20 per cent of all ulcers, or, much more commonly, in the duodenum, which make up the remaining 80 per cent.

Stomach, or gastric, ulcers must be taken seriously. They can be the next step on from gastritis, which is when local areas of the lining of the wall of the stomach are eroded. Unlike gastritis, ulcers don't just occur due to an overproduction of, or imbalances in, acid production. Gastric ulcers can be single or multiple, acute or chronic, large or small. They can appear, heal and leave you in peace then re-emerge again suddenly. The acid production is often normal or even reduced in people who suffer stomach ulcers, so the problem seems more likely to stem from the mucus not being able to withstand the normal acidic conditions in the stomach. This might be because it has been under constant attack from irritants, such as aspirin and alcohol.

Gastric ulcers can cause discomfort once in a while or can, at the other end of the spectrum, lead to excruciating pain if the ulcer perforates and penetrates into surrounding tissues or organs. Pain associated with stomach ulcers usually sets in around one to one and a half hours after eating.

There is no strong consensus on 'natural' causes of ulcers. They do seem, however, to run in families, occur in people with type O blood and in those who push themselves hard at work and often play as well.

There is a growing consensus in the medical world that a large number of ulcers are caused by an infective agent, a bacteria called *Helicobacter pylori*. Work carried out in Australia by Dr Barry Marshall and his team of researchers revealed that, on average, *H. pylori* is present in 65 per cent of patients with stomach ulcers and 85 per cent with duodenal ulcers. However, *H. pylori* is present in the stomachs of many people who don't have ulcers, so the link between this bacteria and ulcers is not quite clear. It could be that people carrying *H. pylori* get ulcers by an unfortunate quirk of their biochemical make-up. If this is so, it would fit in with the observation that ulcers tend to affect members of the same family.

It is known that certain drugs used for arthritis – non-steroidal anti-inflammatory drugs (NSAIDs) – can, unfortunately, lead to perforation of the stomach wall, as can large, continued doses of aspirin.

Ultimately, drugs will probably be needed to heal the ulcer. Various modern drugs are highly effective and are discussed in Chapter 6. However, diet and lifestyle can contribute to the relief of symptoms and help in the healing process.

Dietary Advice

The good news is that the old-fashioned diets of bland foods based on milk and milk puddings and strict dietary programmes have not been proven to be effective in the treatment and management of gastric ulcers, so there is no need to restrict yourself to these kinds of uninspiring choices.

For years, it was believed that milk somehow neutralized an 'acid stomach'. Tests have shown that milk has only a passing neutralizing effect on gastric acids and is actually rapidly followed by a rise in acidity. So, it seems that those who spent long periods on a bland diet of white fish, mashed potato and milky drinks did so in vain. Such a regimen *doesn't* help to heal ulcers.

There are some general guidelines which can be followed as part of a modern gastric diet:

- meals should be small, frequent and regular
- very hot or very cold foods should be avoided as they encourage air to be swallowed, which aggravates the problems
- fried foods should be avoided
- leave out any pickles, black pepper, vinegar, spices and mustard
- avoid tea, coffee, colas, cold remedies with caffeine and alcohol, which all stimulate acid production
- according to herbalists, liquorice has a soothing action on mucous membranes and is often given to help treat ulcers (it can be taken as a drink by pouring hot water over a liquorice root and allowing to simmer for 15 minutes; see Chapter 6).

While consumption of alcohol can rarely be identified as the cause of an ulcer, wine and drinks with 5 per cent or more alcohol are potent stimulants of gastric acid secretion and should therefore be avoided by those with ulcers.

Caffeine again rears its head. Like alcohol, most studies have revealed that while it doesn't *cause* ulcers, it can exacerbate pre-existing conditions. Tea has been shown to have a similar effect after just 200 ml (⅓ pint) has been consumed, which is just a couple of mugs.

B_6 is a vitamin found in meat, milk, potatoes and other vegetables. Some ulcer sufferers have been found to have low levels of this vitamin circulating in the blood. It has been suggested that supplementing with B_6 vitamin could help in the healing of ulcers. The same is true of observational studies on gastric ulcer patients who have taken vitamin C supplements.

Foods rich in vitamin C include all citrus fruits, such as oranges and grapefruits and their respective juices, berries, like strawberries, raspberries and blackberries, kiwi fruit, peppers including red, yellow and green, green leafy vegetables, sweet potatoes, parsley and, in smaller amounts, parsley and ordinary potatoes.

Modest supplements of both vitamins B_6 and C could be considered, but check with your doctor before taking them.

Some research has shown that when laser therapy was given to a group of people with gastric ulcers, it was more effective when given together with vitamin E supplements.

Vitamin E is found in good amounts in wheatgerm oil, and other vegetable oils, wholegrain cereals, eggs, dark green leafy vegetables, such as spinach and dark green cabbage, and sprouts. Avocados are also a good source, as are blackberries.

Taking zinc sulphate supplements has also been looked into and seems to have a degree of success in some people with gastric ulcers. Note, though, that it is easy to take too much zinc, so don't take this supplement without checking amounts with your doctor.

Oysters are the best, and unfortunately the most expensive, source of zinc. Red meat is the next best, however, with lean beef and lean pork boasting the highest amounts. Cheddar cheese is also rich in zinc, as are the dark meat from chicken, lentils, wholegrain cereals, rice and maize.

Work has also been carried out on the effect of essential fatty acids (EFAs) on gastric ulcers. Both those found in vegetable oils, such as sunflower, safflower and evening primrose, as well as those from oily fish, like salmon, tuna, mackeral, sardines, kippers and pilchards, have been indicated to have a positive effect.

It seems that the EFAs in the vegetable oils may enhance ulcer healing. The theory behind their role lies in the fact that EFAs are converted in the body into hormone-like substances known as prostaglandins. Various pieces of evidence indicate these prostaglandins may play a physiological role in protecting the gastric mucous membranes. Supplementing with EFAs in the form of evening primrose oil (Efamol) and fish oils may help protect against and treat ulcers.

There is some evidence that high-fibre diets may be of benefit – not in the healing process, but in delaying the time of another ulcer occurring. This is an area in which further study is needed, but, as a high-fibre diet is essentially a healthy way of eating and will help to provide the nutrients mentioned above, for example B_6, zinc and vitamins C and E, it is certainly worth following such a diet.

Foods rich in fibre include wholegrain breads, wholegrain cereals, like brown rice and pasta, and breakfast cereals such as bran flakes, All Bran, Weetabix, Shredded Wheat, porridge and muesli. Pulses, vegetables and fruit are also good sources.

There is not enough proof from these research findings for dietitians to recommend particular strategies based on them to patients, but they are continuing areas of interest and more remains to be found out and confirmed. A healthy diet plan, such as those given in Chapter 7, will provide plenty of the vitamins and minerals mentioned as well as some of the EFAs.

Duodenal Ulcers

These are ulcers that develop in the very first part of the small intestine and seem, unlike stomach, or gastric ulcers, to be a result of overproduction of acid in the stomach. They can also develop as a result of the stomach emptying too much of its acidic contents into the duodenum in one go, and the duodenum having insufficient alkaline secretions present to neutralize them. The bacteria *H. pylori,* mentioned above, may play an important role in the development of duodenal as well as stomach ulcers.

Like gastric ulcers, duodenal ulcers occur when there has been erosion of the mucous membranes. They may be single or multiple, superficial or deep.

Duodenal ulcers seem to be strongly hereditary – probably because the overproduction of acid runs in families. They are far more common than stomach ulcers. The finger of blame can, once again, in part, be pointed at stress. This was seen clearly to be the case in London during the Second World War where the number of people with ulcers increased dramatically during the air raids. The theory goes that excessive nerve stimulation increased acid production, which led to duodenal ulcers developing. While air raids are a thing of the past, it's easy to see how the pressures of modern life could easily lead to a similar end result. Tight deadlines, frantic schedules, combining family responsibilities with work, bringing up children, financial and emotional worries, combined with other day-to-day problems can create untold stress.

Dietary Advice

Similar dietary guidelines apply for duodenal ulcers as stomach ulcers.

Researchers have tried treating duodenal ulcers with apple pectin (the substance in fruit that makes jam set). When patients were given around 12 mg a day, the pectin seemed to help prevent relapses. The researchers suggest that apple pectin could therefore be used as a form of treatment to help reduce the risk of recurring duodenal ulcers. This treatment is not widely used, however, and so should be talked through with your doctor.

A generally high-fibre diet may, as with stomach ulcers, help reduce the risk of further duodenal ulcers occurring. Research with patients who have duodenal ulcers has shown a dramatically lowered incidence of recurrence in those who follow such a diet, which, some researchers believe, could be because of the increased amount of chewing high-fibre diets require. The extra chewing means more saliva is produced. Saliva is, you will recall, alkaline. The increased flow of this alkaline fluid into the stomach helps lower stomach acidity and, thus, reduces the risk of irritation to the mucous membranes there. Whether or not this theory is true, a high-fibre diet has many other benefits with regard to problems with digestion and so is worth adopting anyway (for details of such a diet, which is also low in fat, see Chapter 7).

Continuously high alcohol intakes seem to cause more duodenal ulcers than gastric ones and so should be avoided wherever possible.

Tea and coffee should also be kept to a minimum so as to avoid encouraging extra acid to be secreted in the stomach.

To avoid developing or to recover from duodenal ulcers, you should follow a low-fat diet. Some fats are necessary as they contain vitamins A, D and E and EFAs. The ones that provide such nutrients are the vegetable and fish oils. Saturated animal fats – found in fatty cuts of meat, the skin of poultry, butter, full-cream dairy products and in manufactured products like pies, pastries, cakes, biscuits and so on – need to be cut right back, and the fats which are eaten need to come from vegetable oils, nuts and seeds and oily fish.

There could be a need for EFAs to be taken as supplements. It has been found that men suffering from duodenal ulcers have significantly lower amounts of the EFA linoleic acid in their abdominal walls than do healthy men. As the amount of linoleic acid stored in fat in the body reflects the amount that is eaten, it would seem that duodenal ulcer sufferers have a lower intake than non-sufferers. As mentioned under Gastric Ulcers, above, the linings of the mucous membranes may be protected by prostaglandins, substances made from linoleic acid. A good supplementary source of EFAs that the body can easily turn into prostaglandins is evening primrose oil.

Gallbladder Problems

When the gallbladder starts producing gallstones, eating can become a complete misery. Soon after indulging in a fatty meal or even just a fatty snack, a person with gallstones can experience severe flatulence along with gripping chest pains. So, what is the gallbladder and why does it cause symptoms of indigestion when it goes wrong?

The gallbladder sits alongside the intestine. It is a thin-walled, small, green, muscular sack or bag that, like a miniature version of the stomach, can expand and contract in size depending on the volume of its contents. It is around 10 cm (4 in) long and can hold between 30 and 50 ml (1 and 2 fl oz), which is about a third of a small yogurt pot. The gallbladder looks a bit like a two-tentacled octopus, with its rounded 'head' connected to both the liver and the top part of the small intestine by two different ducts or tubes.

The gallbladder's function is to store a thick, liquid substance called bile and to release it into the intestine when required. The liver makes the bile and sends it to the gallbladder via one of the ducts. It stays in the gallbladder until the hormone called CCK arrives on the scene, instructing it to shoot bile into the other duct, which leads into the intestine. CCK also has the effect of relaxing the valve located where the duct joins the intestine, thus allowing the bile in.

Bile has one main constituent that helps indigestion – bile salts. Bile salts help break down and emulsify fats in the intestine and distribute them evenly throughout the rest of the chyme. As mentioned briefly in Chapter 1, this is a bit like what happens when milk is homogenized, when the creamy part is thoroughly mixed in with the watery part of the milk, making the fat and water homogenous.

The bile salts, therefore, physically separate the big globules of fat – eaten, for example, in the form of cheese, butter, margarine or ice-cream – breaking them down into millions of tiny fatty droplets.

Bile also contains, among other things, cholesterol and pigments. It is the pigment that gives our stools their character-istic colour. Without bile, they would look a grey white colour and also contain fatty streaks as, without bile, fats are not prop-erly digested or absorbed into the body.

The hormone CCK, which, you remember, stimulates the gallbladder to release bile, is itself released when the contents of the stomach moving into the intestine are rich in fats.

Problems with the gallbladder occur when it makes gallstones from cholesterol. Bile salts normally keep levels of cholesterol at the correct level, but if there is too much cholesterol for the bile salts to deal with, then the cholesterol crystallizes, forming the so-called 'stones'. These sit in the gallbladder itself and/or in the duct, obstructing the flow of bile. When the gallbladder or duct contracts in response to a fatty meal, the sharp crystals dig into the walls and cause agonizing pain, which spreads throughout the right side of the chest region, causing severe indigestion.

Gallstones are known to be a complication associated with obesity. It is well worth shedding excess weight to help avoid developing them (for details of a reducing diet, see Chapter 7). Also, people who are overweight experience worse symptoms when they have gallstones than do their normal weight counterparts. In the late 1980s, 88,837 women aged between 34 and 59 years were selected for a study and followed up over a 4-year period. They completed detailed food and alcohol intake diaries and their weights were recorded. It was found that there was a link between diet and weight in that the more overweight the women, the more likely they were to develop gallstones. One woman who was 41 and over 25 kg (about 4 stone) overweight went on a 1,000 calories a day diet. Over 15 months, she lost 19 kg (3 stone), during which period her gallstones disappeared. After 19 months, she was down to her ideal weight and her gallbladder was working properly.

It would seem sensible, judging from the picture you can build from this research, that getting down to or keeping to a normal bodyweight is a must to give your gallbladder a chance of working properly.

Gallstones can be surgically removed. It is also possible to dissolve the crystals. Nowadays, however, they are more likely to be treated by ultrasound vibrations, which pulverize, or lasers, which vaporize them.

Dietary Advice

A low-fat diet is often prescribed for people who suffer from gallstones. Its effectiveness has not been completely tried and tested with enough clinical studies to know for certain whether or not it is truly effective. However, it does seem to make sense that if fatty foods stimulate the gallbladder to contract and deliver bile to the intestine, that a low-fat diet will reduce its activity and, thus, discomfort. Very often, it's a case of trial and error when working out just how much fat can be tolerated by an individual, and it is worth experimenting with.

For details of a low-fat diet in which only 30 per cent of the total calories come from fat, see Chapter 7. Most people in the West eat diets with around 40 to 45 per cent of the total calories coming from fat. This needs to be reduced to 35 per cent for normal fit people. If you suffer from gallstones, you could try reducing your fat intake to more like the 30 per cent level of the diet included in this book to see if this helps improve symptoms. For a woman who eats about 2,000 calories a day, 30 per cent of this would be 600 calories. As 1 g of fat contains 9 calories, this would mean that she would need to keep the total grams of fat eaten in a day down to around 67 g (2½ oz). For a man eating a total of 2,550 calories a day, 30 per cent of this would be 765. This would translate into a daily total of 85 g (3½ oz) of fat.

For most people, meat and meat products, like sausages, beef-burgers, meat pies and pasties, the spreading fats, like butter and margarine, cooking oils, full-fat milk and dairy products, such as cheeses, cream and full-fat yogurts, are the main sources of fat in the diet because they are eaten on a daily basis. Fats hidden within other foods, like savoury snacks, pastries, biscuits, cakes and puddings and other desserts, also add a considerable and increasing amount of fat to the diet and need to be carefully controlled when on a low-fat diet.

Over the last few years, there has been an enormous growth in the number of reduced and low-fat products appearing on the supermarket shelves, and these can help enormously when you are following a low-fat plan.

Skimmed milk is now readily available, as are reduced or virtually fat-free dairy products, including yogurts, fromage frais, cheeses, ready-made custards and milk puddings. There are also many low-fat and very low-fat spreads, although if you don't like any of them, just use the minimum amount of butter or a traditional margarine. Low-fat ready meals fill the freezer and chill cabinets, and all kinds of reduced-fat crisps, chips, sausages, burgers, dressings and even ice-creams are now on the market.

The following lists of foods – divided into very low-fat, low-fat, medium- and high- fat categories – can help guide you as to the good and bad foods. However, check before you buy because some reduced-fat products are still, compared to other foods, relatively quite fatty. Reduced-fat Cheddar, for example, is still a medium-fat food.

Very Low-fat Foods (less than 5 g per 100 g/⅙ oz per 4 oz)
- Skimmed milk
- Low-fat yogurt
- Egg white
- Cottage cheese
- Turkey breast, skinless, grilled
- White fish, poached or steamed
- Shellfish, steamed
- All vegetables, including potatoes, cooked without fat
- Salad vegetables, without dressing
- Beans, peas and lentils
- Plain boiled sweets
- Jam and honey
- Sauces and pickles
- Marmite
- Bread
- Pasta

- Breakfast cereals
- Crispbreads
- Meringues
- Jellies
- Custard and rice pudding, made with skimmed milk
- Fruits, fresh, frozen, canned

Low-fat Foods (5–10 g fat per 100 g/⅛–¼ oz per 4 oz)
- Ham
- Lean steak, grilled
- Lean roast beef, leg pork, leg lamb, roast chicken, without skin
- Kidneys, grilled
- Pilchards
- Roast potatoes
- Oven chips
- Cream and thick soups
- Muesli
- Ready Brek
- Soft rolls
- Currant buns
- Sponge, such as Swiss roll
- Trifle
- Ice-cream
- Apple crumble

Medium-fat Foods (containing 10–20 g fat per 100 g/¼–¾ oz per 4 oz)
- Full-fat yogurt
- Boiled eggs
- Feta cheese
- Curd cheese
- Reduced-fat Cheddar

- Lean back bacon, grilled
- Rump steak, fried
- Mince, stewed
- Lean lamb and pork chops
- Chicken, roasted, with skin
- Beefburgers, hamburgers
- Livers, fried
- Cod in batter, fried
- Salmon, tinned
- Sardines
- Fish fingers
- Scampi, fried
- Thick-cut chips
- Olives
- Mars bar
- Toffees
- Cream crackers
- Rich tea biscuits
- Oatcakes
- Ginger nuts
- Wafers
- Rock and madeira cakes
- Doughnuts
- Scones
- Fruit cakes
- Pancakes
- Sponge pudding
- Fruit pies
- Lemon meringue pie

High-fat Foods (containing more than 20 g fat per 100 g/¾ oz per 4 oz)

- Butter
- Margarine
- Cream, all types
- Oils, all types
- Mayonnaise, including low-fat varieties
- Low-fat spreads
- Salad cream, including low-fat varieties
- Peanut butter
- Eggs, scrambled and fried
- Scotch eggs
- Stilton
- Cream cheeses
- Cheddar, Cheshire
- Parmesan
- Edam
- Cheese spreads
- Quiche
- Welsh rarebit
- Streaky bacon, fried
- Lamb and pork chops, with fat
- Roast duck, with skin and fat
- Liver pâté
- Luncheon meat
- Pork sausages
- Sausage rolls
- Pork pies
- Pasties and meat pies
- Taramasalata
- Whitebait, fried
- Chips, deep-fried

- Crisps, normal and low-fat varieties
- Avocados
- Soya beans
- Nuts
- Milk chocolate
- Chocolate biscuits
- Filled wafers
- Custard creams
- Shortbread
- Pastry, all types
- Victoria sponge
- Cream cakes
- Pies
- Cheesecakes

As to other pieces of advice, interestingly it has also been shown that women who skipped breakfast or only had coffee at the start of the day had a greater incidence of gallstones than did those who ate breakfast. So, taking breakfast may help prevent gallstones occurring.

In addition, it has been suggested and observed that frequent consumption of smoked foods also seems to encourage the formation of gallstones. Commonly consumed smoked foods include bacon and smoked mackerel.

The good news, though, is that a moderate intake of alcohol may actually help to reduce the incidence of gallstones.

Cholesterol in the Diet

It is commonly thought that when foods known to be rich in cholesterol, such as egg yolks, fish roe and shellfish are eaten, the cholesterol levels in the blood will rise once the foods have been digested. In fact, scientists have never been able to show that blood cholesterol rises after eating such foods. Most of the cholesterol in the blood is made by the body itself. Levels of cholesterol rise if the diet is rich in saturated fats, found in animal fats, dairy products, coconut oil and coconut cream and foods containing these fats.

The incidence of gallstones in France, India, Japan, Portugal, South Africa, Sweden and Uganda was studied back in 1978 and the results showed that in those countries where total calories and fat intakes were lower and vegetable intakes higher, few people had gallstones. After the Second World War, the incidence of gallstones increased in France over a 20-year period. The increases occurred as the diets increased in total calories and fats.

Studies that compared vegetarian women with non-vegetarian women have revealed that, as a group, vegetarian women have less than half the incidence of gallstones of their meat-eating sisters. The researchers carrying out the study believed that this finding could be attributed to the fact that the vegetarians ate less fat and more fibre.

From this it is clear that to help reduce cholesterol levels in the body, it is necessary to keep consumption of saturated fats well down. Eating foods rich in so-called 'soluble fibre' found in, for example, pulses, apples and oats, helps keep cholesterol levels down too.

Irritable Bowel Syndrome

This seems to be the digestive scourge of the 1980s and 1990s. In Britain, it accounts for anything between 33 and 70 per cent of all referrals to gastrointestinal clinics. Everyone knows someone who has irritable bowel syndrome (IBS). Its symptoms usually include abdominal pain, distention of the abdomen and alterations in the stools, varying from being constipated to having really loose stools or, indeed, swinging between the two (see Figure 8). Obviously, such symptoms are distressing, uncomfortable and worrying.

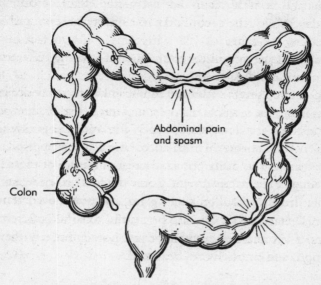

Figure 8 The large intestine of an IBS sufferer.

IBS has been identified as being related, in some women, to the premenstrual time of the month, and it is also often said to be brought on by stress. The one common link between all IBS sufferers, though, is that no physical ailment, such as Crohn's disease, ulcerative colitis, diverticulitis or cancer, can be identified. A great deal of specialist hospital time and equipment is necessary to eliminate all these other possible causes of the symptoms. Only after all the examinations have been carried out on the gut, and no such underlying cause can be detected, can a true diagnosis of IBS be made.

Defining what is normal for the bowels has always been a moot point. Some people can pass stools twice a day and think it is normal, while others could go three days and not consider themselves to be constipated. Some may always feel bloated after eating and consider it to be just a side-effect of eating and drinking, while others may find it uncomfortable enough to seek help. The incidence of IBS symptoms could in fact be even higher than the figures currently quoted as some sufferers may well never seek help or advice.

IBS is not a single entity and can be linked to many situations. Stress from, for example, divorce, moving house, losing a job or the death of someone close, hyperventilation, musculoskeletal problems and hormonal imbalances have all been cited as causes. That there are so many potential causes means that there is not one single effective treatment. Some doctors prescribe antispasmodic drugs, others bulking agents and some even tranquillizers. Dietary advice can also be helpful to some sufferers. IBS provides yet another example of just how intimately the gut's reactions and emotions can be linked.

Dietary Advice

Those who have specific symptoms of abdominal distension and wind may find that cutting out vegetables of the brassica family, such as cabbage, Brussels sprouts and broccoli, and pulses, such as red kidney, baked and black-eyed beans, as well as lentils, peas and chickpeas, and apples, grapes and raisins may help.

In the past, high-fibre diets have been recommended for IBS sufferers. Additions of up to 7 g (about ⅛ oz) a day of wheat bran has, for example, been suggested for people who are suffering constipation as a result of IBS. Today, however, there is a movement away from bran, in recognition of the fact that intolerances to certain foods could be more to blame.

In order to detect which foods may be causing a specific person's problems, an exclusion diet needs to be followed. Research has proven that this has been effective in treating between 48 and 67 per cent of IBS patients. The exclusion diet developed in Cambridge at Addenbrookes Hospital is based on the plan set out below, but note that any kind of exclusion diet should only be undertaken with the permission of your GP and the guidance of an SRD. This is necessary because it is not just a case of leaving out certain foods. It has to be done in a structured way and one that will provide meaningful results. The diet followed during the exclusion period and any diet prescribed afterwards for maintenance must be nutritionally adequate for the person concerned and this needs to be worked out with a qualified SRD.

This is followed for two weeks and then the symptoms are

Foods	Not Allowed	Allowed
Meat	Preserved meats, bacon, sausages	All other meats
Fish	Smoked fish, shellfish	White fish
Vegetables	Potatoes, onions, sweetcorn	All other vegetables
Fruit	Citrus fruits	All other fruit
Cereals	Wheat, barley, oats, corn, rye	Rice, tapioca, millet, buckwheat
Oils	Corn oil, vegetable oil	Sunflower, soya, safflower, olive oils
Dairy	Cows' and goat's milk, butter margarines, yogurts, cheese, eggs	Soya milk, milk-free margarine
Beverages	Tea, coffee, fruit squashes, grapefruit juice, alcohol, tap water	Herbal teas, apple, pineapple, tomato juices, mineral water
Other	Chocolate, yeast, vinegar, preservatives	Carob, salt, herbs, spices, sugar, honey

reassessed. This needs to be done by your doctor. If there has been no improvement, then the person will be advised to return to their normal diet. If symptoms have cleared, however, the foods that were excluded are reintroduced, one at a time at two-day intervals in the following order:

- tap water
- potatoes
- cows' milk
- yeast
- tea
- rye
- butter
- onions
- eggs
- oats
- coffee
- chocolate
- barley
- citrus fruits
- corn
- cheese
- white wine
- shellfish
- yogurt
- vinegar
- wheat
- nuts
- preservatives.

When following such a plan, you need to keep a really close check on your symptoms and write them down on a daily basis.

Just to reinforce the point made above, though, it is vital that this kind of food exclusion diet is followed under the supervision of your doctor and an SRD, who can ensure that the diet is kept to and that the food eaten is sufficiently rich in nutrients for your personal requirements to avoid any adverse effects of the exclusion.

After the results of the exclusion period and reintroduction of foods are known, how you should mix the foods that have been found to be well tolerated will also need to be worked out with an SRD to make sure that your diet will be providing all the necessary nutrients to maintain good health. It's no good having a diet that relieves the symptoms of IBS but is deficient in essential vitamins or minerals as such deficiencies will manifest themselves as problems in the future, such as anaemia from iron deficiency or osteoporosis (brittle bones) due to a lack of calcium.

Research, again carried out in Cambridge, showed that the following foods created symptoms of intolerance in the following percentages of patients:

- wheat, 60 per cent
- corn, 44 per cent
- milk, 44 per cent
- cheese, 39 per cent
- oats, 34 per cent
- coffee, 33 per cent
- rye, 30 per cent
- eggs, 26 per cent
- butter, 25 per cent
- tea, 25 per cent
- citrus, 24 per cent
- barley, 24 per cent
- yogurt, 24 per cent

- chocolate, 22 per cent
- nuts, 22 per cent
- onions, 22 per cent
- potatoes, 20 per cent
- preservatives, 20 per cent.

'Alternative Testing'

It is possible to have a wide range of tests done that claim to prove food intolerances for IBS and other problems. Vega machines, hair analysis, cytotoxic tests and the list goes on. None have any scientific justification. Immunological abnormalities occur in some patients with known food intolerances. These can be detected by means of special tests, but they are notoriously tricky to do and can be unreliable (see RAST and skin tests in Chapter 3).

Some scientists believe that food intolerances can develop due to a change in the flora in bowels due to antibiotic treatment in the past. Changes in flora have indeed been found in IBS patients who identify an aggravating food, remove it from the diet and then reintroduce it. Testing stools for changes in flora to detect food intolerances is not yet a recognized technique and it remains to be seen whether it could become so in the future.

The only reliable dietary treatment method available at the moment is that of following a proper exclusion diet under medical and dietetic supervision, such as the one suggested above.

Constipation

As mentioned in relation to IBS, whether or not you consider yourself to be constipated is very much a matter of personal opinion. None the less, it is still reasonably easy to define. In general terms, it is the delayed transit of faeces, resulting in them becoming hard, dry, small and difficult to pass (see Figure 9).

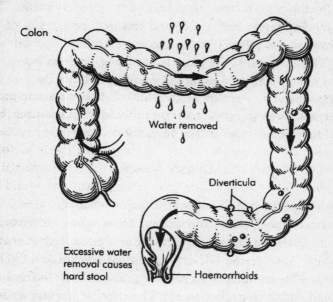

Figure 9 The large intestine of someone suffering constipation.

Constipation has two main causes. One is continually ignoring the need or call from the body to defecate. Doing this will eventually lead to the mechanism becoming less sensitive, with constipation being the result. The other main cause is small faeces. Faeces usually weigh between 75 and 200 g(3 and 7 oz), of which 50 to 175 g (2 to 6 oz) is water. Thus the bulk of the faeces is water and so the ability to hold water is crucial to their final weight. Diet can play a large role in increasing faecal weight by increasing their water-binding abilities.

As with so many indigestion problems, once again the gut-brain link plays a part. Depression, for example, is a frequent

cause of constipation. Pregnant women are also prone to constipation, possibly because the weight of the foetus, pushing the
uterus down on to the colon, delays bowel movements. The
elderly commonly suffer, too, and this may be a result of the
neuromuscular reflexes in the colon becoming impaired with
age. This means that the brain is not being made as aware that
faecal matter is there waiting to be passed out as is the case in a
younger person. They are often guilty of delaying going to the
toilet, too, even when they feel they should. This is especially so
for elderly people who are not very mobile.

Dietary Advice

Increasing the physical bulk of the faeces is one way in which to
help overcome or avoid constipation. Diets rich in fruits, vegetables and wholegrain cereals provide the body with plenty of
insoluble fibre. In the UK, the current average intake of fibre is
around 12 g (about ¼ oz) a day – 6 g (about ⅛ oz) less than the
recommended 18 g (about ¾ oz). The effect of diet on the faeces
and how long they take to travel through the gut was shown by
the research work carried out in the 1970s by a well-known fibre
research expert, Professor Dennis Burkett.

He found that in the group of people from the UK who ate a
typical British diet with lots of refined carbohydrates and therefore not much fibre, the food took around 83 hours to travel
through the entire gut. The daily weight of the stools each
person produced was, on average, 104 g (about 4 oz).

On the other hand, a group of Ugandan villagers who lived on
an entirely unrefined diet containing a lot of fibre had transit
times of 36 hours and produced 470 g (1 lb) of stools each a day.

Interestingly, he found that vegetarians in the UK who ate a
mixed diet, some of which was unrefined, halved the transit time

of their omniverous counterparts and more than doubled their stool weights.

There seems to be a very clear relationship between the composition of the diet and the speed with which the food moves through the gut. Soft, voluminous stools are much easier to pass and help to reduce problems further up the tract. Straining to pass stools over long periods, can, for example, exert pressure higher up in the digestive tract. It can cause pressure all the way back in the stomach and force the top stomach valve open, allowing its acidic contents to reflux back up into the gullet, causing heartburn and inflammation of the oesophagus. Also, such back pressure can affect the diaphragm and eventually lead to a hiatus hernia, which in turn pushes up the stomach and also causes gastric reflux.

A high-fibre diet is generally a healthy way of eating and also helps avoid constipation, but always check with your doctor that there is no underlying cause of constipation in your case and seek his or her approval regarding your going on a high-bulk diet. The diets in Chapter 7 have been designed to provide the necessary 18 g (about ¾ oz) of fibre a day. However, bear in mind the points that follow too when you are building on these diets.

Easy Steps Towards a High-fibre Diet

Always use wholegrain cereals where possible. This means wholemeal bread – not 'brown', but 100 per cent wholemeal. If you cannot tolerate this, try some of the white loaves with added fibre, like Mighty White or Champion, or Granary, which is another possible choice. Brown pasta and brown rice should be used instead of white. If this is unpalatable, try a half-white, half-brown mix. Eat 100 per cent wholewheat breakfast cereals, too, such as bran flakes, Shreddies, All Bran, Weetabix, Shredded Wheat or porridge.

The carbohydrate part of meals should be the central part, with other foods being added to this. Have, for example, a large serving of potatoes, rice or pasta and add to this a smaller portion of protein, such as meat, poultry, fish, eggs, cheese or pulses and nuts. This combination then needs to be accompanied by a large portion of vegetables, salad and or fruit.

One crucial point to remember, however, is that all this will be in vain – and, indeed, have the opposite effect and clog you up – if it is not taken along with plenty of fluids. At least eight cups or glasses of fluid are needed a day in tandem with this highly unrefined diet to ensure that the stools will be soft and easy to pass. Cups of tea and coffee, juices and squashes all count towards this total eight. If you have a high-fibre diet and consume insufficient fluids, your stools end up looking and feeling like a cooked sausage that has been allowed to cool overnight. In other words, hard and difficult to pass, which is the opposite of what you want.

Diarrhoea

Again, the issue of toilet habits must be considered and the distinction made between normal, regular motions and acute or chronic diarrhoea. True diarrhoea is the frequent passing of loose or watery, unformed stools. It may happen suddenly and just occur once in a while or be a problem that continues over a period of time. Diarrhoea happens as a result of a problem in the small and/or large intestine.

The powerful effect of the nervous system on the gut has been mentioned several times so far, and diarrhoea is one of those symptoms everyone can associate with nerves. Pre-exam worries, big decisions, life-changing events, all are more than enough to trigger overactivity of neuromuscular connections, which speeds up peristalsis (the pulsating movement) of the intestinal walls and increases secretions, causing food and water to charge full-speed through the small and large intestines almost undigested.

Diarrhoea can also be the result of irritation or inflammation of the mucous membrane of the bowel by bacterial, viral, proto-zoal, chemical or physical agents. Diseases such as Crohn's disease and ulcerative colitis, as well as problems like gastroen-teritis, also lead to frequent bouts of diarrhoea, which are hard to treat.

Obviously, it will be necessary to consult your doctor and find out the cause of the diarrhoea. If it *is* an on-going problem asso-ciated with a condition such as Crohn's or irritable bowel disease, solutions can be sought on an individual basis. If certain foods trigger it off, the intolerance needs to be investigated and identified with the help of a doctor and an SRD. People often simply then avoid eating foods that tend to trigger off attacks.

Self-inflicted diarrhoea can occur where there is laxative abuse.

Whatever the cause, when sudden and large amounts of very loose stools are passed, above 1,000 g (2¼ lbs)a day, as well as water, huge amounts of water, sodium and potassium are lost, more than can be made up by eating and drinking normally. It is essential that the lost salts and water are replaced to prevent dehydration. If they are not, then irritability, fatigue, drowsi-ness, muscle cramps, thirst, loss of appetite, nausea, headache and faintness soon follow. A home remedy to replace the fluids and salts can be made up by taking 150 ml (¼ pint) boiling water and dissolving in this ½ teaspoon of salt and 4 heaped teaspoons of sugar. Add 150 ml (¼ pint) of fresh orange juice and then make up to 500 ml (17 fl oz) with water. This should be given in small quantities and at frequent intervals. Alternatively, commercial preparations such as Dioralyte can be used and are available from pharmacists and chemists.

It is vital that severe diarrhoea is investigated by your doctor if it persists.

Dietary Advice

As a rule, a bulky diet – in other words, a high-fibre diet – can, surprisingly, often be of help at such times. Instead of aggravating the system and rushing gut contents through at even greater speed, it can help bind the stools up a bit, making them bulkier and therefore slowing them down.

CHAPTER THREE

Food Allergies and Intolerances

During the 1980s, food allergies and intolerances became the focus of much attention. If something went wrong with virtually any part of the body, there was someone willing to relate it back to, and put the blame on, a certain food or drink. While we aren't quite so quick to blame colourings, preservatives and sugar at the first sign of hyperactivity or blotchy skin, some people undoubtedly do react adversely to certain foods or substances in foods.

Intolerances to food and drink fall into several categories and can genuinely affect different body systems, including the digestive system, the skin, blood, bones and so on.

Allergies

A truly allergic reaction to a food or drink when it is consumed means that the immune system responds and sets up an allergic response. There are four types of allergic responses:

1) within a few minutes, usually urticaria (a rash), eczema, asthma, bronchial problems and a runny nose occur
2) a local reaction happens in the cell membrane
3) after a few hours, the skin and bronchi, therefore breathing, are affected

4) around 24 to 48 hours later, the symptoms develop, which are similar to those of the first type, with breathing difficulties being the main one.

The digestive tract is not directly affected by these true allergic responses to food, although it is involved in the digestion and absorption of it.

Tests for Food Allergies

It is very hard to accurately diagnose food allergy. A number of tests exist, some of which may be of use, while others are fanciful, expensive and shed little real light on the situation.

The so-called RAST test (which stands for radioallergosorbent test), involves giving an amount of the suspected allergy-causing food and measuring the antibody response to it. It is quite accurate, but is not foolproof and only certain extracts from foods likely to cause an allergic reaction are available to use as test material.

Skin tests can be used, which involve pricking, scratching or puncturing the skin and applying a given a substance or injecting it just under the skin. This is done to see if the substance causes a weal or redness, which would be taken to indicate an allergy to it. Again, like the RAST test, this is not 100 per cent accurate and some false results may be given in some cases.

After RAST and skin testing, you start entering the realms of the controversial types of testing. These are not available on the NHS and are very expensive. The cytotoxic food test is one such system. This looks at blood samples, but has not been proven accurate. Studies where the same blood sample has been sent under two different names have come back with different results, and when samples from people with true and proven allergies were sent in, their allergies were not identified.

Hair and nail tests are equally hit and miss. It is true that levels of minerals can be detected in hair and that poisons can also be found, but there is no evidence that hair and nail samples can reveal allergies.

Pulse testing is similarly flawed, the diagnosis being based on the pulse rising or not after eating a particular food. It doesn't take into account the wide range of events that cause the pulse to speed up, such as simply having it measured.

Sublingual testing involves cutting out the suspected food for a few weeks and then putting a few drops of it under the tongue. If there is a reaction, this is taken to indicate that there is an allergic sensitivity to that food. The main problem with this is that if the test is carried out on a truly allergic person, they may go into anaphylactic shock when given the test, which can cause the tongue to swell and even lead to asphyxiation.

Dietary Investigation

The most effective form of investigation remains the exclusion diet. This should, however, never be undertaken lightly or without the approval of your doctor and the help of an SRD.

It must be understood before embarking on them that they are time-consuming, socially disruptive and can be expensive. For some, they help identify an offending food and dramatically improve the quality of life. Others may not be so lucky. As it is possible when introducing foods after a period of exclusion to bring on anaphylactic shock, it is vital to only do this under medical supervision.

There are three main ways in which dietary exclusion can be carried out. The first is to simply exclude a single food or food constituent, either because a dietary investigation by a dietitian suggests it or because the person has found there to be a link between eating a certain food and having symptoms. Like most things in life, this isn't as simple as it sounds. While things like chocolate, shellfish and strawberries are easily avoided, milk, wheat, eggs and certain additives are not as obvious and can be ingredients in a large number of foods. Cutting one of these staples out of the diet can result in a restricted nutrient intake and doing so requires careful planning with a dietitian, who will also take into account likes and dislikes of the foods not containing the allergen. This is particularly vital when it comes to children who are growing rapidly and must have an especially nutrient-rich diet.

The second is a multiple exclusion diet, and this is used when a dietary cause is suspected but cannot be identified for certain. This tends to involve cutting out foods people most often react to, such as milk and dairy products, eggs, grains, especially wheat, and, to a lesser degree, nuts, coffee, citrus fruit and chocolate. Azo dyes, used to colour foods and certain fish, can be problematical for some children. The multiple exclusion diet is often followed for two to three weeks.

Foods usually excluded in multiple exclusion diets are:

- milk and milk products
- eggs
- wheat
- citrus fruits.

Foods sometimes excluded are:

- pork, bacon, liver and offal
- fish and shellfish
- barley, oats, corn, rye

- nuts and pips
- yeasts
- potatoes, tomatoes, onions and garlic
- chocolate
- coffee/tea
- food colourings, especially azo dyes
- food preservatives, especially benzoates and sulphites
- soya.

Foods usually allowed are:

- beef, lamb, turkey, rabbit
- rice
- sugar, treacle, syrup
- lard
- vegetables, except potatoes, tomatoes, onions and garlic
- fruit, except citrus ones.

If improvements are noticed, foods have to be carefully reintroduced. The whole process can be very time-consuming and can be beset by many problems, not least of these being the substances hidden in non-foods, such as toothpaste, chalks, crayons and cosmetics, which can be partially ingested during ordinary use.

The third option is the most restrictive of all exclusion diets – the few foods diet. It comprises a small number of foods rarely associated with any reactions. It usually includes:

- turkey and rabbit
- carrots, cauliflower, sweet potatoes and broccoli, but not onions, sweetcorn, tomatoes, soya or potatoes
- rice cakes, rice, tapioca, sago, buckwheat

- pears and peaches, but no citrus fruits
- sunflower, safflower, olive and rapeseed oils
- milk-free margarine, such as Tomor, Vitaquel, Suma or DP Pure
- tap, mineral or soda water
- salt, sugar, syrup, treacle, honey
- milk substitutes for infants and young children.

Again, this diet should not be followed for more than two to three weeks and foods need to be gradually reintroduced under medical supervision in case of a strongly allergic reaction. Vitamin and mineral supplements need to be taken during this kind of exclusion diet to avoid the possibility of any deficiencies occurring. An SRD would advise as to which types of supplements it might be advisable to take.

Maintenance Diets

Once the foods to which there is a sensitivity have been identified, a considerable amount of guidance and support is needed to ensure that the final diet to be followed to avoid these is nutritionally balanced and is actually possible to follow. Factors like lifestyle, shopping facilities, cooking skills and equipment and the number of meals eaten outside of the home, at school, work and so on, need to be taken into account.

One of the odd things about food allergies is that they can pass. Even after just six months, it may be possible to reintroduce the previously offending food with no ill effects. Children in particular often grow out of their allergies to dairy, egg and wheat products.

The Prevention of Food Allergies in Children

Families with a strong history of allergy may be able to help their children avoid similar problems. Foods that trigger eczema and asthma in their parents, for example, can be exluded by the mother while she is pregnant and while breastfeeding. They can also be avoided for at least the first year of life. Breastfeeding seems to give some protection from allergies to the baby. Mothers who have a history of allergies who choose not to breastfeed may be advised to give their babies an infant soya milk in preference to a cows' milk-based infant formula. There is evidence that delaying the introduction of highly allergenic foods until at least eight months of age may be beneficial.

Intolerances

A wide range of reactions to food and drink, some of which do affect the digestive system directly, fall into this category. Some of the mechanisms involved are understood, some remain unexplained.

Non-allergic Histamine Response

The symptoms that occur are similar to the first type of allergic reaction mentioned above, but as no immune system response is involved, the body doesn't release antibodies. Shellfish and strawberries can cause such reactions.

Lactose Intolerance

This occurs when there is a lack of the enzyme lactase in the small intestine, which is needed to break down the milk sugar, lactose. All newborn babies have enough of this enzyme to cope with lactose in breast milk or that found in infant formulas. After weaning, however, lactase activity decreases in all mammals, including man. Lactase levels usually drop between the ages of two to five, so a child may start having symptoms of intolerance as late as when they first go to school. Lactose intolerance can start in later life, too, developing, for example, following a gastrointestinal disease that has damaged the mucosal lining of the tract.

Often lactose intolerance will not be absolute and the person can cope with small amounts. Classic symptoms of lactose intolerance will manifest themselves in the functioning of the digestive tract. Unabsorbed lactose moves from the small intestine into the large and here it will pull in a lot of water and sugar from the blood vessels supplying it. This will lead to diarrhoea. In addition, the lactose is fermented in the large intestine, producing gas. The abdomen usually then swells and is uncomfortable. Children often complain of recurrent abdominal pain.

The doctor should check out such symptoms and eliminate the possibility of there being any other causes of them. If lactose intolerance is diagnosed, then the most effective way of dealing with the symptoms is to go on a lactose-free diet for a period of time specified by your doctor or dietitian, then gradually introduce it to see how much can be tolerated on a day-to-day basis.

Milk and milk products need to be avoided, although fermented milk products can often be tolerated. As dairy products are such a valuable source of calcium, this mineral must be supplied by including other calcium-rich foods.

Calcium-rich Foods

Foods	Mg of calcium per 100 g (4 oz) of food
Tahini	680
Sesame seeds	670
Tofu	510
Spinach	170
Sunflower seeds	110
Ready-to-eat apricots	73
Kidney beans	71
Peanuts	60
Peanut butter	37

Pharmacological Reactions

Some substances in foods when eaten in large enough quantities cause a pharmacological effect, which means that they illicit a specific and direct effect on, for example, the nervous system. Caffeine is one such substance. In small amounts, it is considered by many to have a positive effect, gently stimulating the nervous system and perking you up. In large amounts, however, the effects are less positive. It stimulates increased acid production and output in the stomach, which, if it is empty when this happens, can lead to gastritis. Caffeine in excess also stimulates the heart rate, causes palpitations, sweating and can trigger migraines. Other related substances, like tyramine (found in red wine, blue cheeses, processed cheeses, game and meat extracts), have similar effects and it may be best to take them in moderation.

Irritant Effects of Foods

Volatile and essential oils from spices and flavouring agents can cause direct irritant effects on the wall of the gut from the oesophagus to the stomach and small intestine. They can physically burn the linings of the tract and stimulate glandular secretions.

Monosodium glutamate is the sodium salt of the amino acid glutamic acid. It is added to savoury dishes to improve and enhance flavours. Glutamate is naturally present in seaweeds, Parmesan cheese, shiitake mushrooms and soya beans, and has been used as a natural flavour enhancer for generations. The use of the manufactured form of it – MSG – in Chinese food led to a furore in the UK in the 1970s and 1980s when it was said to be responsible for Chinese Restaurant Syndrome, a set of symptoms including gastric problems, hot flushes, increased heart rates and headaches following consumption of food to which it had been added. It is more likely, though, that such reactions were due to intolerances of other ingredients in Chinese food, such as shellfish and cooked rice that had not been stored in the right way.

Food Aversions

Avoiding certain foods for psychological reasons is possible in childhood and adult life. A food is deliberately avoided because of its associations with, perhaps, a time of sorrow, sickness or some similar unpleasant time. The symptoms of psychological intolerance are usually unpleasant bodily reactions, such as vomiting or some upset with the gut because of the emotions associated with the food that has been eaten. Foods that have been forced on a child at school, for example, can cause someone to be sick at the thought of or on eating it later in life. This kind of reaction brings us back once again to the very fine balance between the brain and the gut. See section on Nausea.

Coeliac Disease

It's hard to know exactly where to place coeliac disease because its real root cause is still unknown. What is known is that it has something to do with the protein gluten, found in wheat and other cereals such as barley and possibly oats, too. Explanations as to what causes it have ranged in turn from gluten being intrinsically toxic to coeliacs because they lack a detoxifying enzyme, to the disease being an allergic reaction by the gut wall to the gluten. Neither theory really explains why it strikes over a wide range of ages or why different symptoms are experienced.

The effect, whatever the cause of the intolerances, is clearly known. The tiny finger-like projections, the villi, which cover the walls of the small intestine become eroded so that the intestinal wall becomes flattened. The absorptive area is thus drastically reduced and so undigested material whizzes through, leading to one of the most obvious symptoms, changes in the stools. They may become either large, pale and smell offensive or become loose, later develoing into diarrhoea. Vomiting may also occur.

In children, a normal baby who is weaned onto foods containing gluten will start by refusing foods and then begin to lose weight. The child will become listless, the stools become as described above and the abdomen will swell, developing into a pot belly.

In adults, the classic symptoms of indigestion can be the first signs of gluten intolerance. These could be anything from abdominal fullness, discomfort in the stomach region, diarrhoea or pain to vomiting. The changes to the stools may be the main tell-tale sign as they become pale, bulky and dreadfully smelly. This is because fat is not being absorbed by the flattened intestinal walls so it remains in the faeces.

Treatment for the disease is to avoid gluten in the diet as much as possible. There are two main sources. The obvious sources are foods made from wheat flour or which contain barley or oats – bread, cereals, cakes, biscuits, pies and pastries, for example. Second, there are the less obvious sources. These are manufactured or processed foods that contain any of these cereals as fillers, thickeners, for bulking up and so on. They may be in the form of gluten, wheat starch, rusk or hydrolysed vegetable protein of wheat origin. They are added to the most unlikely things, such as sweets, as well as slightly more obvious ones, such as white sauces in boil-in-the bag cod in parsley sauce and tinned foods like chicken in sauce.

Gluten-containing foods to avoid	Gluten-free alternatives
Cereals and cereal products	
Wheat, wholemeal, wholewheat and wheatmeal flours. Bran, barley, rye, rye flour, pasta, including all the shapes, and semolina.	Arrowroot, buckwheat, corn cornflour, maize, and maize flour. Gluten-free flour, potato flour, rice and rice flour. Sago, soya and soya flour. Tapioca.
Cereals made from wheat, barley or rye, such as muesli, Shredded Wheat, Sugar Puffs and Weetabix.	Rice Krispies and cornflakes.
Baked products made from wheat, barley, rye flour, suet and semolina.	Gluten-free baked biscuits, bread, cakes and gluten-free pasta.
Crispbreads and starch-reduced bread and rolls. Ice-cream wafers and cones, plus Communion wafers.	
Milk and milk products	
Artificial cream containing flour.	Fresh, dried, condensed,

Yogurt containing muesli.

evaporated, skimmed, sterilized. Fresh or tinned cream. Most yogurts. Cheddar, curd and cream cheeses.

Cheese spreads containing flour, which many do – check the labels.

Egg dishes

Eggs cooked with flour, such as Scotch eggs, eggs with white sauces. Quiches and egg flans.

Cooked without breadcrumbs and sauces.

Fats and oils

Suet contains flour.

All butters, margarines, oils, lard and dripping.

Meat and fish

Savoury pies and puddings made with flour. Any meat or fish with stuffings, breadcrumbs or suet. Sausages and burgers with bread-crumbs or rusk (check the pack-aging) Battered and crumbed fish, like fish fingers and fishcakes.

Plain meat and fish. Plain tinned fish. Check packaging of burgers and pre-packed meat – some are gluten-free.

Vegetables, fruits and nuts

Tinned vegetables in sauces, such as creamed mushrooms. Potato croquettes. TVP containing wheat.

Fresh, tinned, cooked, dried and frozen, pulses and soya. Some baked beans – check the labels.

Fruit in fruit pies, crumbles and cakes.

Fresh, cooked, tinned, dried and frozen.

Nuts in cooked products and

Fresh, plain, salted.

crackers and dry-roasted nuts.

Jams, sweets and desserts

Sweets containing or rolled in flour. Smarties, marshmallows, liquorice and Twix.

Sugar, glucose, jam, honey, marmalade, treacle, molasses, some mincemeat – check the label. Plain ice lollies.

Puddings and desserts with flour, breadcrumbs and suet, such as pies crumbles and summer puddings. Ice-cream cones and wafers.

Jellies and milk puddings made from permitted cereals. Check the labels of ice-cream and instant desserts as some are gluten-free. Not semolina.

Drinks

Barley-based instant coffee, barley-flavoured drinks. Bengers, malted drinks, such as Horlicks. Home-brewed beer, cloudy real ale, and hot drinks from vending machines.

Tea, pure, instant or fresh ground coffee, cocoa, fizzy drinks, squashes, and cordials, fresh fruit juices, wines, spirits, beer and lagers.

Soups, sauces and seasonings

Soups thickened with the cereals wheat, barley, rye or pasta. Bisto.

Home-made soups with suitable thickeners. Certain brands of tinned and dried soups. Certain gravy brownings. Check the packaging.

Some peppers, ready-mixed spices and curry powders.

Fresh peppers and herbs. Check the labels on other seasonings, mustards and powders.

Note: Beware that some medicines contain gluten, so check with the pharmacist or your doctor before taking anything if you are unsure.

If you are diagnosed as having coeliac disease, it is worth joining the Coeliac Society, which provides regular updates on which foods contain gluten. An SRD is also vital in planning a healthy and nutritious gluten-free diet.

Candidiasis

The organism *Candida albicans* is present in the normal healthy gut. It has been claimed by some doctors and researchers that certain people can become sensitive to the normal amounts present and that others can start to overproduce it. In both cases, they believe that *Candida* may be the root cause of certain symptoms of indigestion that have previously been blamed on other causes. The symptoms outlined include abdominal bloating, pains and cramps, diarrhoea, nausea or irritable bowel syndrome.

The American Academy of Allergy and Immunology, however, feels that, at the present time, the concept of candidiasis is, as yet, unproven. The Academy believes that, for the moment, any treatments offered should be seen as experimental and only used in patients who wish to take part in appropriately designed and executed trials.

Some such trials have already been carried out, with interesting results. One experiment, for example, showed that *Candida albicans* fails to grow in human saliva unless it is supplemented with glucose.

A trial was carried out in 1984 in which 100 women who had recurring *Candida* infections of the vagina had the sugar in their urine measured. When sugar appeared in the urine, it related to a time of excessive sugar intake. When sugar was eliminated as much as possible, there was a dramatic reduction in the incidence and severity of the *Candida* infections.

In an experimental study back in 1966, of 255 patients with long-term urticaria, 49 of them reacted to *Candida albicans* antigens, and 55 per cent of them also reacted to brewer's yeast. After treatment with a low-yeast diet and anti-fungal therapy, 27 out of the 49 experienced a clinical cure.

It has been suggested that a diet which excludes simple carbohydrate and yeast-rich foods will prevent candidiasis by depriving the organisms of a suitable environment in which to grow. This kind of diet requires the person involved to avoid foods containing simple sugars, which means no adding of sugar to foods or drinks at the table or eating foods rich in it, such as sweets, biscuits, cakes, ice-creams and desserts, fruit juices, condiments and tinned fruits in syrup. It also involves cutting out yeast-containing foods and drinks, such as malted products, mushrooms, cheeses, peanuts and alcoholic drinks, as well as vinegar-containing foods and vitamin and mineral tablets, unless they are sugar- and yeast-free, and antibiotics.

The debate continues, but there are some respected clinics in which doctors and SRDs working together have seen improvements in patients who follow such diets and take the drug nystatin (prescribed for fungal infections).

CHAPTER FOUR

The Digestive Turmoil of Food Poisoning

Every day the digestive system is presented with 'foreign substances', such as bacteria and natural and chemical toxins, and it generally deals with these effectively and safely, killing them off, detoxifying them or simply coping with their presence. Sometimes, however, a food or drink may contain too much of a particular infectious or toxic agent or be harbouring one against which the body has no defences.

When things get out of balance and poisoning occurs, the digestive tract plays an important role in eliminating the poison, by ejecting it from the system as quickly as possible. It does this by expelling the food from either the top or bottom of the tract by vomiting or diarrhoea. Less drastic symptoms of food poisoning include milder forms of indigestion, such as irritation of the mucous membranes, causing discomfort in the throat and/or the stomach, and feelings of nausea.

There are plenty of natural toxins in food that, in small amounts, we deal with effectively without suffering adverse effects. Ingesting them in large amounts however is a different matter. Solanine – the substance in green potatoes – is one such example.

Potatoes normally contain about 7 mg of solanine per 100-g (4-oz) serving. It is found mostly in green skin, but also in the eyes and sprouts of potatoes. It isn't enough just to cut off the green bits and remove eyes as the solanine can spread throughout the potato. When very small amounts of solanine are eaten, mild forms of poisoning occur that manifest themselves as general gastrointestinal discomfort, such as stomach ache and aches in the intestines, too. As the levels of solanine consumed rise, symptoms of nausea, vomiting and diarrhoea quickly set in. If levels of 33 mg per 100 g are reached, trouble really starts as the nervous system then becomes affected, with fever and the risk of circulatory collapse occurring, too.

It is best to avoid potatoes with any sign of greening or sprouting. Always store them in a cool, dry, dark place to reduce the risk of solanine being produced, which happens when they are exposed to light for more than just a few days.

Toxins in poisonous mushrooms are another cause of vomiting and diarrhoea. *Amanita phalloides* is the mushroom most commonly responsible for poisoning in Britain. If only small amounts are ingested, you may get away with just abdominal pain.

Problems with mussels infected with saxitoxin are more likely than finding a rogue mushroom in your food as there is no way of telling whether or not the mussel on your plate has fed on plankton containing the saxitoxin. Mussels themselves are not affected by it and, as it is not killed by cooking, it is only after eating a 'bad' one that you know because then you will be suffering from severe vomiting and diarrhoea.

As well as naturally occurring toxins, normally healthy foods and drinks can become infected by bacteria, which, once eaten, affect the digestive tract. Bacteria such as salmonella infect the intestines directly, causing upsets and aches, whereas others produce toxins and it is these toxins that do the damage, such as clostridium. The symptoms may be very severe and obviously linked to something recently consumed. Equally likely, however, are much milder levels of infection and these lead to general discomfort in the stomach and gut, feelings of nausea, queasiness and general indigestion, which won't be attributed to food poisoning.

Problems with food poisoning have always existed. The processing food undergoes now in the West attempts to reduce the risk by using a variety of techniques, such as pasteurization, canning and cooking, which all act as safeguards. The storage and handling of food and drink by the industry, retailer and ourselves at home plays a vital role in keeping food poisoning under control.

Common Forms of Food Poisoning

Bacterial

Salmonella

Salmonella is the name given to a group of bacteria, of which there are more than 1,600 types. They are among the most common causes of food poisoning, infecting poultry and many other intensively reared animals. When we eat the infected meat, the bacteria are taken in with the food and usually stay in the intestinal tract where they wreak their havoc, causing pain, diarrhoea and vomiting. This usually begins around 12 to 36 hours after having eaten the contaminated food. It is quite common to be able to trace the symptoms back to a certain meal by checking how the people you ate with are feeling as it is likely that all the people who ate the same food will be similarly affected. The digestive problems will usually last for up to two to three days.

Most cases of salmonella occur as a result of uncooked or badly cooked foods or food that has been cooked and recontaminated. If, for example, an egg custard pie is cut with a knife that has been used for raw poultry and not thoroughly washed before being used again, the egg custard could easily become infected.

People can become carriers of salmonella. They have salmonella but don't have any symptoms, yet can pass the bacteria on to infect and affect others.

Basic Rules for Avoiding Salmonella Contamination

Meat and meat products, poultry, eggs, milk and milk products are the foods most commonly susceptible to salmonella contamination. If they are stored, handled and prepared properly, they do not pose a risk.

- When storing uncooked poultry, it should be kept in a fridge at less than 5°C and in a container that will not allow juices to drip on to foods below.
- Food should always be prepared with clean equipment and this should be thoroughly washed afterwards.
- Food should be cooked for long enough and at the correct temperatures.
- Cracked or damaged eggs should not be used and neither should those past the sell-by date. Dirty eggs should be wiped with a dry, clean cloth, but not washed as this destroys the protective film.
- Unpasteurized milk should be avoided.

Campylobacter

Stomach pains and discomfort followed by diarrhoea and fever are common symptoms of infection with campylobacter. The main type to infect the digestive system is *Campylobacter jejuni*. They are present in foods such as raw milk, some raw meats and poultry and unchlorinated water supplies. Campylobacter do not multiply in food, but once they enter the stomach and gut, they feed on what is for them a nutritionally rich medium that has the requisite low oxygen content and multiply with great speed. The symptoms are seldom serious and it is possible that an unexplained bout of indigestion could be down to mild infections with this bacteria.

The best way to avoid such infection is to only consume pasteurized or UHT milk, only drink water from known sources and avoid cross-contamination between cooked and uncooked foods. Heating does kill the bacteria, so cooked foods eaten hot are usually no problem.

Escherichia Coli

Consuming food or drink infected with *Escherichia coli* (usually simply *E. coli*) will again adversely affect the digestive tract. When the bacteria are ingested, they sit in the intestines and produce toxins, which lead to stomach pains, diarrhoea and maybe vomiting, too. The illness can last from one to seven days. Mild forms may cause cramps and indigestion that does not lead on to severe symptoms.

E. coli live in the large intestine and are transferred to food by means of poor personal hygiene. Simply thoroughly washing hands after going to the toilet and drying them on a clean towel is the best way of stopping them spreading. Meat can be infected with *E. coli* from humans or other animals. Care in handling is therefore vital to prevent infection.

Staphylococcus Aureus

Digestive tract symptoms of infection with *S. aureus* are similar to other types of food poisoning, including stomach cramps, nausea, diarrhoea and vomiting. The uppermost part of the digestive tract can also be affected, with excess saliva being produced. The bacteria produce a toxin that takes effect one to four hours after eating and can last for up to two days. *S. aureus* are found in the nasal passages of humans and animals and also often found in infected wounds and boils. They can also be passed from infected cattle into their milk.

As with *E. coli*, good hygiene can help avoid infections. Keeping hands clean and covering cuts and wounds is essential. Once the toxins have been produced, they cannot be destroyed by heating so preventing them from contaminating the food in the first place is vital. Poultry, meat, fish, milk and milk products are most susceptible to contamination with this bacteria.

Bacillus Cereus

If you become infected with *Bacillus cereus*, you will know about it all too soon. Usually within an hour, the bacteria have produced a toxin that will bring about waves of nausea and general discomfort in the stomach. If the poisoning is bad, sickness will follow within an hour and diarrhoea will start after eight hours.

B. cereus is found in the soil, but can find its way into the food chain. Once in food, the bacteria produce a toxin that actually only does the damage when the food is eaten. Boiled and fried rice are foods commonly affected by this bacteria, especially if cooked in bulk and left to stand for some time at normal room temperature. Custards, cereal products, puddings and sauces can also be affected.

The best way to avoid infection with *B. cereus* is to chill foods as quickly as possible once they have been cooked. Large quantities should be divided up into smaller amounts to speed up cooling and then be stored in the fridge. If reheated, it should be to temperatures above 70°c.

Moulds

Moulds are part of the fungi group of organisms. Most moulds are white and look furry or fuzzy, like fine cotton wool, although some are dark or coloured. Eating mouldy foods can upset the stomach and lead to vomiting and sickness.

Moulds usually turn foods bad and some also produce mycotoxins, which will cause harm when eaten. Some, however, are used in the food industry to make, for example, soy sauce and blue cheeses.

Mouldy foods should be thrown away. Scraping it off does not remove any toxins that may have been produced and have entered the food. Moulds are spread in the air as tiny spores that land on a food and multiply rapidly, which is another good reason for not disturbing it by cutting but simply throwing the whole piece away.

CHAPTER FIVE

You're Not Alone

The number of people who are affected by indigestion is staggering. Just to recap, in the UK alone around 14 million people at any one time experience bloating, aching, bouts of wind and general discomfort on eating, with half suffering at least once a week. Indigestion disrupts work, pleasure and leisure time, enjoyment of food and drink and even sleep. If you suffer from indigestion, therefore, you certainly aren't alone.

A survey of 1,004 people was conducted by NOP Consumer Market Research in October 1994 to find out what proportion of the population suffered, their ages, what types of people they were and what they felt caused their indigestion.

It was found that just over half of these people had experienced indigestion and that there were no differences between the number of men and women who were affected.

In all age groups of people questioned, some people suffered, but those aged between 35 and 64 were most affected. People in professional occupations were most prone to attacks, followed by managerial and manual workers.

Of the people who said that they had had problems with indigestion, 80 per cent could relate it to a particular cause. The foods that were perceived to cause the most attacks, beginning with the most commonly cited, included:

- fatty foods, 58 per cent
- spicy foods, 47 per cent
- alcohol, 39 per cent
- fizzy drinks, 37 per cent
- rich foods, 31 per cent
- onions, 29 per cent
- peppers, 24 per cent
- citrus fruits, 23 per cent
- fruit juice, 20 per cent
- garlic, 17 per cent
- tomatoes, 13 per cent
- chocolate, 13 per cent
- coffee, 12 per cent
- food containing air, 9 per cent
- cabbage, 6 per cent.

Women seemed to be more aware of which particular types of foods triggered their indigestion than were men. Fatty foods, for example, were more frequently pinpointed by women than men. Spicy foods, second on the list, were, again, mentioned more often by women than men.

Alcohol and fizzy drinks came next. Alcohol was the second most common cause stated by men, and, in fact, the only factor mentioned significantly more often by men than women. The difficulties caused by alcohol follow the general trends seen in alcohol consumption. Men and those in work mentioned this cause more often than other groups. The older respondents had less trouble with alcohol sparking off indigestion, which is in line with the general drop in alcohol consumption in this group.

Rich foods were unspecified but acknowledged by a significant number of the people asked to be a contributing factor to their digestive upsets.

Among the individual foods mentioned, onions and peppers were the most frequently pinpointed. The survey revealed that indigestion following eating citrus fruit was more of a problem in older people and they mentioned fruit juices as a cause more often, too. Less frequently mentioned were problems triggered by garlic, tomatoes, chocolate and coffee. Those who thought eating foods with air in them were to blame named popcorn and meringues as potential causes.

The people taking part in the survey were then asked what they avoided because it gave them indigestion. The answers they gave are shown below in perceived order of importance.

Factor	Percentage who avoided it
Overeating/eating too quickly	85
Stress	59
Putting on weight	58
Eating before bed	58
Exercising after meals	55
Tight clothing	51
Eating fast foods	49
Smoking	31
Bending	30

Overeating or eating too quickly is clearly the main factor thought to lead to indigestion. All age groups and social groups agreed on this point and tried to avoid doing this.

There was fairly widespread agreement about the adverse effects of stress on the system, with 59 per cent of respondents trying to avoid it.

The negative effects of putting on weight and eating just before going to bed were acknowledged as well, with 58 per cent of the people asked trying to avoid both problem areas.

Half of the people who took part in the survey said they avoided exercising after a meal, wearing tight clothes and eating fast foods. The likelihood of avoiding fast food due to indigestion increased as social class decreased.

Tight clothing, again, not surprisingly, was much more likely to be mentioned by women than men, probably because fewer men than women wear tight clothing.

Nearly a third avoided smoking and bending because they caused indigestion. More younger people than older ones stated that they avoided smoking as it caused indigestion. Perhaps not surprisingly, older people on the other hand more often avoided bending over and stress.

Other factors people mentioned that they actively avoided were few. Of those which were, alcohol appeared most frequently, but then only 5 of the 1,004 who took part in the survey specified it. Other things that were mentioned as triggering indigestion, all be it by only a few people, were unripe bananas, chicken, coleslaw, fruit, honey, dairy products, tuna, fancy food, fried food, pregnancy and gardening.

These results show that people have quite a good idea as to what dietary and lifestyle factors trigger indigestion.

Women and Indigestion

Another survey carried out by NOP Consumer Market Research in January 1995, that focused on women and indigestion involved talking to 442 female participants. An interesting overview of women's eating habits emerged from the survey.

Women, it seems, respect and value the importance of mealtimes. For example, 80 per cent of those asked manage to put time aside for lunch and even more do so for the evening meal – a total of 90 per cent. Their meals tend to vary in the times they are taken by only one or two hours and consist of meat and vegetables, pasta and fish dishes. Working mums with children were more likely to rely on convenience foods and ready meals.

The results regarding breakfast weren't quite so consistent. Non-working women with no children tend to relax over breakfast, while half of those with children had to grab theirs on the run. Cereal and toast proved to be the clear favourites for breakfast.

Lunches on the whole are approached in a relaxed way, but mothers with young children and working mothers are more likely than other women to have to rush and eat on the go. Sandwiches form the basis of lunch for 91 per cent of working mothers and 85 per cent of non-working mothers.

Snacking is quite common, both mid morning and mid afternoon, and the favourite snacks to have at these times are biscuits, fruit and crisps.

During the day, around 4.5 cups of tea are drunk by women and about 2 cups of coffee. Only 1.5 glasses of water are taken and 0.7 glasses of orange juice.

Of the women surveyed, 186 out of the 442 admitted to suffering from indigestion. A fifth of them had problems with digestion at least once a week. Interestingly, it was the working and non-working women without children who suffered from it most often.

Specific foods that caused problems and triggered symptoms of indigestion included spicy foods – which were the most common trigger, affecting 38 per cent of the women – followed by fatty foods, at 32 per cent, and onions and chocolate, at 17 and 12 per cent respectively.

Family problems lay at the root of stress-related indigestion and included factors such as redundancy and their children, especially young children, who need so much looking after.

Juggling the commitments of work, home and family, particularly when the family includes children and/or an elderly relative, also acted as a key trigger.

This survey reveals that, as with the first one we looked at, which covered a mixed population, women knew how to relieve some of their digestive problems, adjusting their lifestyles and diet.

Stressful Jobs

Taxi Drivers

Unlike the women in the above survey, taxi drivers surveyed at the same time, because of the nature of their jobs, have a very high tendency to skip meals and make up for them with lots of snacks grabbed on the go.

Only just over half the taxi drivers asked have either breakfast or lunch, often delaying mealtimes for up to two hours and compensating with a high volume of snacks and sandwiches throughout the day.

Almost a quarter of all taxi drivers eat lunch in their cabs, with over 95 per cent having a mid-morning snack as they park in their cabs and more than a third eat an afternoon snack while driving.

Taxi drivers reflect the national average, with about a third of them being able to relate symptoms of indigestion to fatty foods, followed by cucumbers and spicy foods. A third of them also felt that sitting in the cab for long periods and eating too quickly, as well as experiencing stress from driving in the traffic, were likely causes of their indigestion. Eating in a cramped space without a chance to walk around afterwards could well exacerabate the problems.

Journalists

Another high-stress job that, contrary to popular belief, the survey revealed, does not involve regular four-hour lunches. Of the journalists questioned, a very different style of eating habits emerged. Far from wining and dining their way through large meals and even larger expense accounts, 78 per cent take lunch at their desks. In addition to this, 27 per cent eat breakfast and 90 per cent of all their snacks at their desks, too. It is the older journalists, those perhaps who can remember times when there *were* long lunches, who try to get out during the day and go to a café, pub or restaurant for a quick bite.

With such a desk-bound daily routine, surprisingly, only half of those who took part in the survey manage to keep to regular mealtimes, with a fifth actually delaying mealtimes by over two hours and a third skipping meals altogether.

Perhaps not entirely surprising, however, is the finding that journalists have a significantly higher problem with indigestion than the national average, with 54 per cent suffering at some stage. Over 60 per cent of this group attribute the causes of their indigestion to eating too quickly while working at their desk, followed closely by the 52 per cent who put it down to the stress and pressure of work. More than a third thought the cause was working long, unsociable hours, having inconsistent mealtimes and eating on the move.

Journalists clearly show how lifestyle factors can be a major cause of indigestion. Just a quick break away from the desk and dedicating 15 minutes to eating at a leisurely pace, followed by a brief walk around could help overcome many of these journalists' problems.

First-hand Experiences

When you're suffering from indigestion at home, work or out for a meal, it may be difficult to imagine that others are going through the same thing. Most of us keep the symptoms to ourselves and learn to find ways of coping without making a fuss. Here, though, some first-hand experiences of indigestion are related, proving that you're *not* alone. You may recognize some of your own experiences in these accounts.

Caroline: 'I've stopped enjoying food in the week'

Caroline is 32 and a buyer for a large store. It's an exciting job, but it involves long hours, a lot of travel and plenty of out-of-hours entertaining. All that is frequently hampered by bouts of indigestion.

If I don't have time for breakfast I don't eat it because I know I'll end up feeling really bloated and uncomfortable for the rest of the morning. It's important in my job to look good.

When I can, I take time for lunch – I'm usually exhausted if I don't. But often I'm eating en route to somewhere or with a client. It's got now that I never enjoy these meals. Partly because I'm nervous, partly because of the rich foods they usually involve, I know I'll get indigestion afterwards – pain in my stomach, bloating, even wind. I hate it. I can honestly say the only time I really enjoy food is at the weekend, when I can eat what I like at my own pace – and not suffer afterwards.

Jean: 'I often get up in the middle of the night because of the pain'

Jean is 60 and a housewife. She says she's suffered from indigestion for about six years, and has got so used to it she expects to feel bad if she goes out for a special dinner or after she's treated herself to a particularly creamy cake or fresh bread. She suffers more at night, and knows that it's linked to her being slightly overweight (she's 76 kg/12 stone), but she doesn't understand why.

I don't think I eat really unhealthy meals. But I know when I do indulge in something very creamy I'll suffer later. But I can't avoid those things forever can I? It's always worse if we go out for a meal in the evening. I often end up getting up in the night because of the pain.

Matthew: 'If I go out with my mates on Friday night, I pay for it'

Matthew is 33 and, at the end of a working week, he likes to meet his friends in the pub for a session. Often they go on from there to the local curry house. It is usually Saturday night before his stomach has settled down.

I'm not exactly ill afterwards – I usually stick to a couple of pints, three or four cigarettes, and the curry we eat is perfectly OK. No one else seems to suffer anyway. But I do feel awful – I know I'll suffer as soon as I've drunk the first pint. Gassy, bloated, uncomfortable. All I want to do is lie down and sleep it off, but when I do, I feel worse. I reckon on at least 18 hours before I feel right again. Surely curry and beer isn't that bad for you!

Katie: 'I stopped enjoying my evening meal because I knew what was to follow'

Katie, 34, was fine until the last few months of pregnancy, when the baby had grown quite large. He pushed up on her stomach so that when it was full after the evening meal and she laid down to go to sleep, reflux was almost inevitable.

I've never suffered with indigestion and used to wonder what all the fuss was about. Then I became pregnant and in the last few months I stopped enjoying my evening meal because I knew what was to follow. I had that dreadful burning sensation in my throat every night. It didn't stop me eating because I wanted to keep up my strength and I wasn't overweight. I can honestly say though that one of the best things about giving birth, apart from our beautiful son, was that I could enjoy eating again. If I put on a lot of weight and that feeling of heartburn was a side-effect of weight gain, then it would be a very good reason for shedding the excess pounds.

It is quite surprising when you start chatting to others just how many people decide that such disruptive and uncomfortable problems are everyday and become an accepted part of the regular routine of things. As more and more information is made known to us about the kinds of foods we need to eat to be healthy, it seems amazing that so little time and mention is made to cover one of the most important parts of a good diet – good digestion. Over and over, it seems that people don't realize the role that different types of foods and drinks play in maintaining a healthy and balanced digestive system.

CHAPTER SIX

๑๑

Indigestion Remedies

Indigestion in its many forms has been with us since time immemorial. Put together the potent forces of food, overindulgence and anxiety and you have the perfect recipe for digestive disorders. It's hardly surprising, therefore, that throughout the history of medicine, remedies have been sought to alleviate symptoms. After Roman feasts, it was common for those who had grossly overindulged to take a concoction to make them vomit. By purging themselves in this way, they helped prevent some of the more painful effects of indigestion, which would have surely followed such huge intakes of food and wine.

Less drastic ways of treating indigestion have been found in the form of herbal remedies throughout the centuries, and, with the ever increasing developments in the modern pharmaceutical industry, many effective drugs are now also available.

The gastrointestinal tract, as we saw earlier, propels, stores, digests and absorbs nutrients and eliminates wastes. The regulation of these activities is achieved by the nerves in the gut, which are linked with the main central nervous system, and by a wide range of gastrointestinal hormones. The problems that can be treated by pharmacological preparations include gastric and duodenal ulcers, constipation, diarrhoea, infections and inflammation. In each case, the potential benefits of treatment must be weighed up against possible side-effects, and the roles of lifestyle and diet must also be taken into account in the overall treatment.

You will recall from earlier discussion the roles that diet and lifestyle can play in maintaining good digestion and alleviating indigestion, but it's important to take a look here at other potential remedies and treatments to complete the picture. Included in this chapter are both herbal and orthodox remedies that may give relief and, in some cases, help prevent certain digestive disorders.

Can Herbal Remedies Help?

Herbs have been used to treat medical conditions for centuries. Before the pharmaceutical industry we have today had developed, physicians relied on natural remedies to treat many conditions. Hippocrates, regarded as the father of modern medicine, knew the properties of 300 medicinal herbs way back in AD 377. Herbalism today still aims to treat and prevent diseases using remedies from plants that can easily be included in our diets. They are usually taken in one of three forms.

1) As infusions – some of the leaves, flowers or stems are covered with a cupful of boiling water, the container is sealed and left for about 10 minutes and then the liquid is strained off and drunk either hot or once it has cooled.

2) As decoctions – roots, twigs, berries, seeds, bark or a combination are put in a pan and cold water is added (25 g/1 oz of material to one cup of cold water). This mixture is then brought to the boil, simmered for 20 to 30 minutes to extract the plant's ingredients, then strained and taken as a drink.

3) Plant material can also be made into cold compresses, juices, ointments and poultices.

Today, as the activities of some plant extracts can actually be analysed, it is being seen that many traditional herbal remedies have a good scientific reason for working as well as they do. Very often in the past people instinctively used certain plants when they were suffering from various ailments. The bark of the cinchona tree, for example, was chewed by South American aborigines to relieve malaria. Centuries later, scientists realized that the bark contains quinine, the substance now used in modern medicine to treat malaria.

In order to get the most out of herbal remedies, it is necessary to consult a herbalist, who will be able to tailor treatment to your individual circumstances, based on your medical history. There are herbs that are well-known for relieving indigestion, however, so it is likely that they will prescribe one or more of these.

It is important never to rely on self-medication – *always* check with your doctor to make sure there are no serious underlying causes for any of your symptoms. If there are not, a herbalist will guide you as to the best way of making use of the following herbs.

An A to Z of Herbs That May Help

Herb	Condition
Angelica	Flatulence
Basil	Appetizer, vomiting, constipation
Camomile	An antispasmodic, the oil is good for stomach cramps
Comfrey	Diarrhoea, stomach ulcers, bleeding gums
Elder	Laxative
Marjoram	Diarrhoea, flatulence, stomach ache

Mint and Peppermint	Flatulence, abdominal aches
Parsley	An antispasmodic
Rosemary	Stomach ache, an antispasmodic, tonic for stomach complaints
Sage	A digestive, antispasmodic, good for nervous diarrhoea, gastritis
Sorrel	A laxative, helps digestion, ulcers in the throat and mouth
Valerian	Good for flatulence

Some Examples of How Digestive Problems Can be Treated with Herbs

Acid Stomach

An infusion of the herb meadowsweet is believed to help soothe the membranes of the digestive tract, including the stomach.

To make the infusion, a cup of boiling water is added to 1 to 2 teaspoons of dried meadowsweet, the container covered tightly and the mixture left to infuse for 15 minutes. The infusion can be drunk up to three times each day.

Taking ginger capsules or a ginger decoction may also help. To make a decoction, take 1½ teaspoons of freshly grated ginger root, cover it with a cup of water, bring it to the boil and simmer for 10 minutes. Strain and drink when needed.

Anxiety

That there is a brain–gut connection is clear from previous chapters. That anxiety and stress can adversely affect the workings of the digestive system is also clear. To relieve anxiety, tension and stress in order to avoid it having repurcussions on your digestion, make an infusion of valerian.

To do this, add 1 to 2 teaspoons of the root to a cup of boiling water. Leave the mixture to infuse for 5 minutes, then strain off the liquid and drink it either hot or once it has cooled down.

Natural Laxatives

Sorbitol

This is a sugar alcohol found in some fruits, such as plums, apricots, cherries and apples, and is made for commercial use from fruit sugars. Sugar-free products for diabetics and sugar-free sweets often contain sorbitol.

Sorbitol is absorbed quite slowly from the intestine and tends to draw water into it. If eaten in large amounts – if a tube of sugar-free mints is consumed in one session, for example – it may lead to stomach pains and diarrhoea.

Prunes

Most fruit bulks up the stools and thereby speeds their passage through the intestines. Prunes, however, also contain derivatives of a substance called hydroxyphenylisatin, which directly stimulates the smooth muscle of the colon wall, setting off a mild form of diarrhoea in susceptible people.

Others

Some other natural foods that seem to exert a laxative effect include:

- rhubarb
- senna
- castor oil
- figs
- molasses
- liquorice.

Common Orthodox Indigestion Remedies

For the Stomach

Until recently, neutralization of the acidic conditions in the stomach had been the only way to deal with indigestion in this part of the tract and this method has been used for several centuries. More recently it has been discovered that it is possible to control the actual production of acid in a very specific way. It is also recognized that in addition to controlling the production of acid, it is worth looking into ways of fortifying the usual protective mechanism of the stomach – the mucous membranes.

Controlling the acidity in the stomach is an important part of the treatment for ulcers and severe acid reflux.

Neutralizing Acids – Antacids

Antacid, literally means anti-acid, and antacid medicines are designed to neutralize the acid in the stomach. The various ones are therefore made from one or more alkaline substances. Liquid preparations work fastest, but tablets are more convenient to carry around.

By neutralizing the acid in the stomach, antacids produce two desirable effects. They decrease the total amount of acid that moves on into the duodenum and stop the activity of pepsin (one of the enzymes in the stomach juices that breaks down protein). Over long periods, all antacids can have side-effects, so they shouldn't be taken for more than two weeks or so. With those you can buy over the counter at your chemist or pharmacist, it is best to check with your doctor before taking them and essential to do so if you are pregnant or breastfeeding, on a low-sodium diet, suffer from heart, blood pressure, liver or kidney problems, or take other medicines on a regular basis.

There are two main types of antacids. Those which are absorbed into the bloodstream and are therefore capable of increasing the pH level of the blood as well as the stomach, which leads to alkaline urine being produced. Then there are the ones that are not absorbed and so do not affect the blood. These are preferable to the absorbed kind if the medicine is to be taken over a couple of weeks.

What is in antacids?

- *Baking soda* Known chemically as sodium bicarbonate or sodium carbonate, these are fast and effective antacids, although they can wear off quickly. They can also lead to belching because they produce carbon dioxide in the stomach. The sodium content makes them out of bounds for anyone with a heart condition, high blood pressure, liver or kidney problems. These antacids are the type that are absorbed into the bloodstream.
- *Chalk* The chemical name for chalk is calcium carbonate. Like baking soda, chalk is an effective antacid. It does release carbon dioxide as it sets to work, however, and can lead to constipation, so it should not be taken for long periods. It is capable of interacting with other medicines like antibiotics, too, so, again, check with your doctor before taking. These antacids are not absorbed into the bloodstream.
- *Aluminium hydroxide* This is less effective than the two

above. Like chalk, it has a constipating effect, so it is usually available in a preparation that also contains magnesium, which has a laxative effect so they cancel each other out. This type of antacid must be avoided if you have kidney problems and is known to interact with some antibiotics, antifungal drugs, warfarin and digoxin.

- *Magnesium carbonate, magnesium trisilicate, magnesium hydroxide* These are effective antacids, but they have a laxative effect. They are usually found in combination with calcium or aluminium and are another type that should be avoided if you have kidney problems.

These are the main active ingredients in antacids, but they also contain other ingredients to help relieve various symptoms.

- *Dimethicone or simethicone* This is added to help break up the gas bubbles, although there is little really good evidence regarding its effectiveness. It is supposed to work by allowing the gas bubbles to coalesce (join together) and then be expelled.
- *Alginic acid* This comes from seaweed and, when it reaches the stomach, forms into a foamy gel. This gel works by sitting as a raft on top of the stomach's contents, preventing them from refluxing out of the stomach and back up into the oesophagus.

Antacids are useful for helping ulcers to heal, if taken properly. Their disadvantage is that they have to be taken regularly and, as mentioned, have side-effects. The chalky taste most of them have is often poorly accepted, which means that people tend to stop taking them before they have had their beneficial effect and healing has been completed. It would seem that antacids are not as safe as some of the newer treatments, which actually stop the acid being produced in the first place.

Blocking Acid Production

How acid is produced and secreted into the stomach was described in Chapter 2, but, to refresh our memories, it is controlled by several mechanisms.

1) Nerve stimulation, which can be triggered by the sight, smell and taste of food and its arrival in the stomach. The particular nerve involved is the vagus nerve, which releases a substance called acetycholine and this fixes on to a special receptor site in the acid-secreting parietal cells in the stomach wall. This action then stimulates acid secretion.

2) By a hormone called gastrin. Gastrin is released from the mucous membranes of the stomach when food is present. The gastrin latches on to its own special gastrin receptor sites in the parietal cell to stimulate acid secretion.

3) By the action of a substance called histamine, which itself is stimulated by the presence of food in the stomach and by acetylcholine and gastrin. Histamine latches on to a histamine receptor in the acid-secreting parietal gland.

When just one of these three stimulators fixes on to the parietal cell, the secretion of acid is scanty. When all three fix on to it, though, the acid literally pours into the stomach.

Mechanisms to reduce acid secretion therefore involve blocking the substances that cause the parietal cells to release it. These are the following.

Anticholinergics

These drugs stop the impulses from the vagus nerve getting to the acid-secreting cells in the stomach wall. They are able to reduce acid secretion but do not stop it completely.

Anticholinergics were known to have various side-effects. For example, some people found they developed blurred vision, others developed a dry mouth, making chewing and swallowing difficult. Small doses may still be used, but, in the main, they have been replaced by the following more modern treatments.

H_2 Antagonists

These substances are able to latch on to the histamine receptor site on the parietal cell and effectively prevent the histamine latching on. If no histamine is locked on to the receptor, the parietal cell will not release any acid. It's rather like blocking someone's keyhole up with filler or glue – there is then no way for them to get their key into the door and thus turn it to enter. H_2 receptor blockers, or antagonists, as they are called, include substances with names like famotidine, cimetidine and ranitidine and block all three stimulators of the acid-secreting cell.

H_2 blockers work by reducing the background level of acid during the day and night in the stomach, as well as the amount of acid that is released during the day in response to eating and drinking, and even just thinking about food. The decrease in acid secretion that results from this blocking allows the mucous membranes, in particular the duodenal ones, to tolerate the lower acidity of the material it receives from the stomach, which gives the ulcer a better chance of healing, improves the speed at which healing occurs and helps prevent the recurrence of ulcers.

Side-effects of these medicines are usually rare and minor, although people with kidney problems do need to take them in lower doses. There can also be interaction with other medication, like warfarin, so, again, care needs to be taken.

The H_2 receptor sites are not the same as the histamine

receptor sites in the airways and air passages – these are H_1 sites. These are not therefore affected by the H_2 antagonist drugs used to treat indigestion.

Proton Pump Inhibitors

Once the sites on the parietal cell have been locked on to whether it is by acetylcholine, gastrin or histamine, all then go on to cause hydrochloric acid to be secreted into the stomach by a pump action. There is a group of drugs that can interfere with this final part of the process so that even if the receptor sites have been stimulated, acid production can still be stopped. These drugs are called proton pump inhibitors.

They produce a more rapid response and promote a faster rate of healing of ulcers than H_2 antagonists and are particularly good for people suffering from refluxing up into the throat or oesophagus. They can, however, cause side-effects, including headaches, rashes and diarrhoea.

Antibiotics

Since the emergence of the theory that stomach ulcers may be caused by the bacteria *Helicobacter pylori* (*H. pylori*), many doctors now treat stomach and duodenal ulcers with a cocktail of drugs. Such a cocktail would include an antibiotic, taken for a week or two, to eradicate the bacteria, and an H_2 blocker, such as cimetidine, famotidine or ranitidine to control acid secretion and give the ulcerated region a chance to heal. Such treatment seems to work very effectively.

Mucus-protecting Agents

Another group of substances can help, too – the cytoprotectants. They act by increasing the secretion of the protective mucus and bicarbonate, and/or by actually providing a physical barrier, thus covering up the ulcer, preventing further irritation of the area to aid healing.

Sucralfate, for example, is thought to act by coating the ulcer, by forming a sticky substance which protects against acid, pepsin and bile salts. It also stimulates the production of mucus, bicarbonate and prostaglandins. It is effective in helping the healing of ulcers.

Another long name to remember is carbenoxolone sodium. This helps the healing of gastric and duodenal ulcers along by improving mucosal defence. It is not the usual first choice in ulcer treatment because of the availability of other more modern drugs that have effective track records. Carbenoxolone sodium is not suitable for children, pregnant women, the elderly or those with heart, kidney or liver problems.

Pharmacy Availability of H$_2$ Blockers

Doctors have been able to prescribe H$_2$ blockers for some years. Some well-known ones are Tagamet (cimetidine), Zantac (ranitidine) and Pepcid (famotidine). However, it is now possible to buy weaker versions from the chemists as an 'over-the-counter' product – in other words, you ask the pharmacist for it. The pharmacist should run through a checklist before allowing you to have it, though, to check that it is safe for you to take. These products are called Tagamet 100, Pepcid AC and Zantac 75.

Many of the medicines that have been mentioned are available from your doctor on prescription. However, there is a bewildering range of indigestion remedies on offer at pharmacies and chemists. See the Appendix for a list of the common ones available and what their active ingredients are.

CHAPTER SEVEN

The Diets

There are three diet plans in this section and the aim is for them to help in the following ways.

1 The Antiheartburn Diet

This first diet is for people who suffer from heartburn. The daily food intake is based on the calories needed by an average woman aged between 19 and 50, which works out at around 1,900 day. The diet has been designed to provide three small meals and two snacks a day. This helps to avoid overfilling the stomach, thus greatly lessening the chances of reflux. It also attempts to avoid all those foods known to make heartburn worse by weakening the valve at the top of the stomach. These foods exclude onions, garlic and many spices, so the recipes have been flavoured with lots of fresh herbs to keep meals tasty and enjoyable. The diet also excludes other valve weakeners, such as caffeine, mints and chocolate.

The Antiheartburn Diet provides an overall healthy balance of nutrients. The recipes try to ensure that no more than 35 per cent of the overall calories come from fat, and all are rich in starchy carbohydrates. They contain adequate protein and are also good sources of micronutrients, such as vitamins C and the B complex ones, as well as the minerals calcium and iron.

The meals in this section could easily be eaten by all adults wishing to follow a nutritious, balanced diet.

2 The Low-fat Diet

This second diet is for those people who are trying to stick to a low-fat plan to help keep gallbladder problems under control. It has again been designed to provide 1,900 calories a day. In this diet, the meals are very much main meals and snacking in between is kept to fruit. The dishes all provide under 30 per cent of their calories from fats, with the exception of one lamb dish that is just over this level. Once again, care has been taken to ensure that a good intake of vitamins and minerals is maintained and a high intake of fibre, which may help prevent gallstones recurring.

3 The Reducing Diet

The third diet provides 1,300 calories a day and is designed for people who want to lose weight slowly and carefully but don't want to stop enjoying what they are eating and drinking. The meals have all been planned to fit in with general healthy eating guidelines and extra care has been taken to make sure that, while the total number of calories is fewer than you would normally consume, the diet is still packed with all the other nutrients you need. If you feel you want to take a one-a-day-type vitamin and mineral supplement while on the diet, it won't do any harm.

Note for all the Diets

For all the recipes, the number of calories and grams of fat provided per serving are given. The percentage of the calories that come from fat are also given in brackets. It is agreed that a healthy diet should consist of foods and meals that ensure you get 35 per cent of the calories from fat, 50 per cent from carbohydrate and 15 per cent from protein, and all the diets provide you with these elements in these proportions.

The nutritional information given with each of the recipes has been calculated from the metric measures for the ingredients. So, although we have tried to be as accurate as possible when giving the imperial conversions of the metric measures, it is necessary in so doing to round figures up or down and therefore the figures given for calories and grams of fats will be approximate if you use the imperial measures. However, the differences are slight, so you can still be sure that you are eating as healthily as possible if you prefer to use the imperial measures.

The Antiheartburn Diet

The meals from each section can be put together in whichever way you choose, to suit your lifestyle and when in the day you prefer to eat main and light meals. Don't feel obliged to try all the dishes – you can just stick to those you enjoy. Most people, for example, don't have a different breakfast every morning, but the choice is there should you feel like a change. As the lunches and dinners have the same numbers of calories, they can be swapped over if you normally eat your cooked meal at midday.

Whichever meal you have in the evening, always be sure to eat a good two hours before going to bed.

When following The Antiheartburn Diet, it is best to have no more than two cups of weak tea and weak coffee a day, preferably less. You can use decaffeinated versions of both. Alternatives include Barley Cup or Caro as well as dandelion drinks, mint and camomile herbal teas. For soft drinks, avoid colas and chocolate drinks and try to have water instead. It's best to avoid all acidic and sugary soft drinks, too.

As mentioned above, the average woman needs to consume 1,900 calories on a daily basis. Men need about 650 more and can gain these extra calories by having larger portions of bread, potatoes, rice and pasta in the recipes given, plus an extra snack and piece of fruit.

The total daily calories are divided to provide your body with a little food often during the day as follows:

- breakfast, 400
- snack, 200
- lunch, 400
- snack, 200
- dinner, 400

making a total of 1,600 calories a day.

The remainder of the calories are accounted for as follows:

- 600 ml (1 pint/2½ cups) of milk, 200
- an extra piece of fruit, to be eaten when desired during the day, 100

making a grand total of 1,900 calories.

Breakfasts

Porridge with Raisins, Plus Wholemeal Toast and Marmalade

398 CALORIES

10 G (¼ OZ) FAT (23 PER CENT)

30 g (1 oz) porridge oats	⅓ cup oatmeal
230 ml (8 fl oz) skimmed milk	1 cup skim milk
2 tsp raisins	2 tsp raisins
2 ready-to-eat apricots	2 ready-to-eat apricots
1 tsp brown sugar	1 tsp brown sugar
1 thick slice wholemeal bread	1 thick slice wholewheat bread
1 tsp low-fat spread	1 tsp low-fat spread
1 tsp marmalade	1 tsp marmalade

Make up the porridge using the skimmed milk according to the instructions on the pack. Once cooked, stir in the raisins and apricots and sprinkle with the brown sugar.

Toast the bread and serve with low-fat spread and marmalade.

Baked Banana with Fromage Frais and a Toasted Muffin

398 CALORIES

9 G (¼ OZ) FAT (20 PER CENT)

1 large banana, peeled	1 large banana, peeled
1½ tsp dark brown sugar	1½ tsp dark brown sugar
1 tbsp mango juice	1 tbsp mango juice
2 tbsp low-fat fromage frais	1 tbsp low-fat fromage blanc

1 wholemeal muffin, sliced in half	1 wholewheat English muffin, sliced in half
2 tsp low-fat spread	2 tsp low-fat spread

Pre-heat the oven to 200°C/400°F/gas 6.

Take a rectangle of foil large enough to wrap the banana in loosely. Lay the banana on the foil, sprinkle with the sugar and mango juice, then scrunch up the foil around the banana and bake in the pre-heated oven for 10 minutes. Unwrap and serve in the foil with the fromage frais.

Follow the baked banana with the muffin, toasted, topped with the spread.

All Bran with Grated Apple, Granary Toast and Marmalade

403 CALORIES
6 G (⅛ OZ) FAT (14 PER CENT)

55 g (2 oz) All Bran	Scant cup All Bran
1 medium apple, grated	1 medium apple, shredded
150 ml (¼ pint) skimmed milk	½ cup skim milk
1 thick slice Granary bread	1 thick slice graham bread
1 tsp low-fat spread	1 tsp low-fat spread
1 tsp marmalade or honey	1 tsp marmalade or honey

Put the All Bran in a bowl and cover with, or mix in, the grated apple. Pour over the skimmed milk and serve.

Toast the bread and serve with the spread and marmalade or honey.

Grilled Mushrooms on Sunflower Seed Toast with Chilled Carrot and Celery Juice

397 CALORIES
9 G (¼ OZ) FAT (21 PER CENT)

4 flat mushrooms
2 thick slices wholegrain bread
with sunflower seeds or
wholemeal bread
2 tsp low-fat spread
Salt and freshly ground
black pepper
Pinch of celery salt
200 ml (⅓ pint) carrot juice,
chilled

4 flat mushrooms
2 thick slices wholegrain bread
with sunflower seeds or
wholewheat bread
2 tsp low-fat spread
Salt and freshly ground
black pepper
Pinch of celery salt
Scant cup carrot juice,
chilled

Wipe the mushrooms clean and grill. Toast the bread, spread the low-fat spread over, arrange the mushrooms on the toast and season to taste.

Stir a pinch of celery salt into the carrot juice and serve.

Boiled Egg with Bread, Bread with Marmalade and Iced Mango Juice

394 CALORIES
13 G (½ OZ) FAT (30 PER CENT)

1 egg
2 slices wholemeal bread

1 egg
2 slices wholewheat bread

2 tsp low-fat spread	2 tsp low-fat spread
1 tsp marmalade	1 tsp marmalade
200 ml (⅓ pint) mango juice, chilled	Scant cup mango juice, chilled
2–3 ice cubes	2–3 ice cubes

Boil the egg and serve with a slice of the wholemeal bread, spread with half of the low-fat spread.

Have the second slice of bread topped with the rest of the spread and the marmalade.

Crush the ice cubes in a tea towel with a wooden rolling pin (or just use whole) and place in a tall glass. Add the chilled mango juice and serve.

Blackberry Fruit Shake and Toasted Fruit Loaf

401 CALORIES
8 G (¼ OZ) FAT (17 PER CENT)

100 g (4 oz) blackberries, fresh or frozen	Scant cup blackberries, fresh or frozen
Small pot of low-fat plain yogurt	Small pot of low-fat plain yogurt
200 ml (⅓ pint) skimmed milk	Scant cup skim milk
2 slices fruit loaf	2 slices raisin bread

Defrost the blackberries if using frozen. Blend together the blackberries, yogurt and skimmed milk. Serve chilled in a tall glass.

Either toast the fruit loaf slices or have them untoasted, as you prefer, and serve them with the shake.

Muesli-topped Yogurt and Peach with Honey-roasted Sunflower Seeds

400 CALORIES
12 G FAT (½OZ) (26 PER CENT)

40 g (1½ oz) unsweetened muesli	¼ cup granola
1 peach, chopped	1 peach, chopped
3 tbsp low-fat plain yogurt	3 tbsp low-fat plain yogurt
2 tsp honey-roasted sunflower seeds	2 tsp honey-roasted sunflower seeds
150 ml (¼ pint) skimmed milk	½ cup skim milk
1 slice wholemeal bread	1 slice wholewheat bread
1 tsp low-fat spread	1 tsp low-fat spread

Put the muesli in a bowl, add the peach and yogurt and sprinkle the sunflower seeds over. Pour the milk over the top to serve.

Follow with the bread, toasted and topped with the spread.

Mid-morning Snacks (each around 200 calories)

201 calories
3 g (⅛ oz) fat (13 per cent)
   2 Jaffa Cakes and 1 medium banana.
194 calories
6 g (⅛ oz) fat (30 per cent)
   2 digestive biscuits (graham crackers) and 1 medium apple.
197 calories
2 g fat (30 per cent)
   2 slices malt loaf and 1 peach.
191 calories
5 g (⅛ oz) fat (21 per cent)

1 currant bun (raisin bun) and 50 g (2 oz/scant ½ cup)
strawberries or other soft fruit.

202 calories

7 g fat (⅛ oz) (29 per cent)

1 wholemeal fruit scone (wholewheat raisin biscuit) and 2
fresh apricots.

201 calories

4 g (⅛ oz) fat (17 per cent)

2 crispbreads (wholewheat crackers) and 30 g (1 oz)
reduced-fat Edam.

197 calories

8 g (¼ oz) fat (36 per cent)

1 thick slice wholemeal (wholewheat) toast and 30 g (1 oz)
cream cheese.

Lunches (each around 400 calories)

Lentil Soup with Wholegrain Roll and Raspberries with Fromage Frais

404 CALORIES

14 G (½OZ) FAT (31 PER CENT)

220 g (8 oz) tinned lentil soup	1 cup canned lentil soup
1 wholegrain roll	1 wholegrain roll
60 g (2½ oz) fresh raspberries or fruit of your choice	½ cup fresh raspberries or fruit of your choice
60 g (2½ oz) plain fromage frais	¼ cup plain fromage blanc

Heat the soup and serve with the roll.

Wash the raspberries and serve in a bowl topped with the
fromage frais.

Watercress Soup and French Bread with a Nectarine

396 CALORIES

4 G (⅛ OZ) FAT (8 PER CENT)

2 bunches watercress
A few fresh tarragon fronds
550 ml (18 fl oz) water
Salt and freshly ground
black pepper
115 ml (4 fl oz) skimmed milk
120 g (4½ oz) chunk
French bread
1 medium nectarine

2 bunches watercress
A few fresh tarragon fronds
2¼ cups water
Salt and freshly ground
black pepper
½ cup skim milk
4½ oz chunk French bread

1 medium nectarine

Put the watercress and fresh tarragon in a pan. Add the water, season to taste, bring to the boil and simmer very gently, covered, for 25 minutes.

Blend, then add the milk and simmer for 10 more minutes. Check the seasoning, allow to cool, then chill.

Serve a quarter of the soup with the French bread. Chill or freeze the rest of the soup.

Have the nectarine for dessert.

Chicken Roll with Lettuce and Peppers and a Peach with Ice-cream

399 CALORIES
14 G (½ OZ) FAT (32 PER CENT)

1 wholemeal roll	1 wholewheat roll
1 tsp low-fat spread	1 tsp low-fat spread
80 g (3 oz) cooked chicken	3 oz cooked chicken
Freshly ground black pepper	Freshly ground black pepper
2–3 lettuce leaves	2–3 lettuce leaves
3 rings red pepper	3 rings red bell pepper
1 tsp reduced-fat salad cream	1 tsp reduced-fat salad cream
or mayonnaise	or mayonnaise
1 medium peach	1 medium peach
60 g (2½ oz) ice-cream	2½ oz ice-cream

Split the roll and spread the low-fat spread on the lower half. Lay the cooked chicken on top. Grind over some black pepper, then add the lettuce and pepper rings. Spread the salad cream or mayonnaise on the other half of the roll and place on top of the filling.

For dessert, slice up the peach and serve with the ice-cream.

Bean and Pasta Salad with an Orange

402 CALORIES
3 G (⅛ OZ) FAT (7 PER CENT)

75 g (3 oz) wholemeal macaroni	¾ cup wholewheat macaroni
1 carrot, grated	1 carrot, shredded
1 stick of celery, finely diced	1 stick of celery, finely diced
2 tbsp tinned chickpeas, drained	2 tbsp canned garbanzos, drained
Salt and freshly ground	Salt and freshly ground
black pepper	black pepper
½ small pot of plain yogurt	½ small pot of plain yogurt
2 sprigs fresh parsley,	2 sprigs fresh parsley,
chopped, to garnish	chopped, to garnish
1 orange	1 orange

Cook the macaroni according to the instructions on the pack. Drain and leave to cool.

Stir the carrot, celery and chickpeas into the cooled macaroni. Season to taste, then mix in the yogurt. Sprinkle the parsley over and serve.

Have the orange for dessert.

Beef Club Sandwich and an Apple

400 CALORIES
6 G (⅛ OZ) FAT (20 PER CENT)

1 tsp low-fat spread	1 tsp low-fat spread
3 slices wholemeal bread	3 slices wholewheat bread

45 g (2 oz) cooked lean roast beef	2 oz cooked lean roast beef
1 tsp horseradish sauce or to taste	1 tsp horseradish sauce or to taste
1 tsp reduced-fat salad cream or mayonnaise	1 tsp reduced-fat salad cream or mayonnaise
1 lettuce leaf, washed	1 lettuce leaf, washed
4 slices cucumber	4 slices cucumber
1 apple	1 apple

Use the spread on one slice of bread. Place the roast beef on top and spread with the horseradish sauce to taste. Lay the second slice of bread on top of this. Spread the salad cream or mayonnaise on this piece of bread and lay the lettuce and slices of cucumber on top. Add the final piece of bread, hold firmly and cut diagonally into four. Put a cocktail stick through each quarter to stop the sections toppling over.

Have the apple for dessert.

Cottage Coleslaw with Pitta

400 CALORIES
6 G FAT (⅛ OZ) (13 PER CENT)

100 g (4 oz) white cabbage, shredded	1 cup shredded white cabbage
1 medium courgette, grated	1 medium zucchini, shredded
1 orange, peeled and chopped	1 orange, peeled and chopped
100 g (4 oz) cottage cheese	½ cup cottage cheese
2 tbsp low-fat plain yogurt	2 tbsp low-fat plain yogurt

Freshly ground black pepper
1 pitta bread

Freshly ground black pepper
1 pitta bread

Mix together the cabbage and courgette. Add the orange and cottage cheese and stir in the yogurt. Season with black pepper to taste. Cut the pitta bread in half crossways and make a pocket. Use the Cottage Coleslaw to fill the pitta pockets.

Greek Salad with Hot Bread and a Pear

400 CALORIES
12 G (¼ OZ) FAT (28 PER CENT)

40 g (1½ oz) feta cheese, cubed
4 black olives, stoned
2 tomatoes, chopped
1-in (2.5-cm) chunk of cucumber, diced
1 tbsp oil-free French dressing
80-g (3-oz) chunk French bread
1 small pear

1½ oz feta cheese, cubed
4 black olives, pitted
2 tomatoes, chopped
1-in chunk cucumber, diced
1 tbsp oil-free French dressing
3-oz chunk French bread
1 small pear

Put the feta cheese into a bowl with the olives, tomatoes and cucumber. Pour the French dressing over and mix. Warm the bread and serve with the salad.

Have the pear for dessert.

Mid-afternoon Snacks (each around 200 calories)

Jam Sponge

196 CALORIES
3 G (⅛ OZ) FAT (15 PER CENT)

Have a 65 g (2½ oz) slice of jam-filled Swiss roll (jelly roll) with a cup of tea or coffee.

Fruit and Nut Snack

203 CALORIES
11 G (¼ OZ) FAT (47 PER CENT)

Mix together 10 g (¼ oz/1 tbsp) of hazelnuts with 10 g (¼ oz/1 tbsp) of peanuts and 30 g (1 oz/2 tbsp) of raisins and serve.

Chocolate Spread Bread

198 CALORIES
6 G (⅛ OZ) FAT (22 PER CENT)

Spread a thick slice of wholemeal bread with 1 tablespoon of chocolate spread and serve.

Milky Barley Cup and Biscuits

207 CALORIES
7 G (⅛ OZ) FAT (28 PER CENT)

Heat 220 ml (7 fl oz/scant cup) skimmed milk and stir in 1 tablespoon of Barley Cup or other drink of your choosing. Serve with 2 digestive biscuits (graham crackers).

Oatcakes with Banana

199 CALORIES
5 G (⅛ OZ) FAT (5 PER CENT)

Mash, chop or slice a medium banana and put it on to 2 oatcakes. Alternatively, simply eat the banana with the oatcakes.

Rice Pudding with Fruit

195 CALORIES
0.5 G FAT (2 PER CENT)

Chop 3 fresh apricots and stir into a pot of ready-made, low-fat rice pudding.

Fromage Frais with Apple Chunks

202 CALORIES
7 G (⅛ OZ) FAT (30 PER CENT)

Chop 1 medium apple and add the chunks to the contents of a small pot of plain fromage frais (fromage blanc) spooned into a bowl. Crumble 2 biscuits (cookies) of your choice over the top for an enjoyable crunch.

Dinners (each around 400 calories)

Hamburger and Salad in a Bun with Chips

PER SERVING: 400 CALORIES
10 G (¼ OZ) FAT (22 PER CENT)

SERVES 1

55 g (2 oz) very lean minced beef	2 oz very lean ground beef
Salt and freshly ground black pepper	Salt and freshly ground black pepper
Worcestershire sauce, to taste	Worcestershire sauce, to taste
Pinch of dried mixed herbs	Pinch of dried mixed herbs
120 g (4½ oz) oven chips	4½ oz oven chips
1 hamburger bun	1 hamburger bun
1 lettuce leaf, washed	1 lettuce leaf, washed
1 tomato, sliced	1 tomato, sliced
4 slices cucumber	4 slices cucumber
Ketchup, to serve, if desired	Catsup, to serve, if desired

Put the mince in a bowl and season to taste with salt, pepper and a dash of Worcestershire sauce. Add a pinch of mixed herbs and mix well. Form into a burger with your hands and grill both sides until well cooked right through.

Meanwhile, cook the oven chips according to the instructions on the pack. Slice the burger bun and toast the insides until they have just lightly browned.

Place the grilled burger on the bun and add the lettuce, tomato and cucumber. Serve with the oven chips and some ketchup, if you can tolerate it.

Cauliflower Cheese with Green Beans and Strawberries and Ice-cream

PER SERVING: 406 CALORIES
15 G (½ OZ) FAT (32 PER CENT)

SERVES 4

400 g (14 oz) fresh cauliflower
480 g (1 lb) new potatoes, scrubbed
2 tbsp low-fat spread
25 g (1 oz) flour
600 ml (1 pint) skimmed milk
Freshly ground black pepper
Pinch of celery salt
100 g (4 oz) reduced-fat Edam cheese, grated
360 g (¾ lb) green beans
2 sprigs fresh parsley, chopped
440 g (1 lb) strawberries, hulled, washed and halved
4 x 60-g (2½-oz) scoops ice-cream

14 oz fresh cauliflower
1 lb new potatoes, scrubbed
2 tbsp low-fat spread
¼ cup all-purpose flour
2½ cups skim milk
Freshly ground black pepper
Pinch of celery salt
1 cup shredded reduced-fat Edam cheese
¾ lb string beans
2 sprigs fresh parsley, chopped
1 lb strawberries, hulled, washed and halved
4 x 2½-oz scoops ice-cream

Break the cauliflower into florets, cook in a little water, drain and keep warm in a flameproof serving dish.

Put the potatoes on to boil. While they are cooking, make a cheese sauce by melting the low-fat spread in a pan over a medium heat and adding the flour. Stir well for 3 minutes, then remove from the heat and gradually add the milk, stirring all the time. Season to taste with black pepper and celery salt. Stir in the

Edam and wait until it has all melted. Pour the cheese sauce over the cauliflower and brown under a hot grill. Also, lightly cook the green beans.

Garnish the cauliflower cheese with the chopped parsley and serve with the potatoes and green beans.

For dessert, serve the strawberries with ice-cream.

Baked Tuna Broccoli

PER SERVING: 405 CALORIES
13 G (½ OZ) FAT (29 PER CENT)

SERVES 4

4 medium baking potatoes	4 medium baking potatoes
180 g (6 oz) tinned tuna in brine, drained and flaked	Scant cup drained and flaked canned tuna in brine
180 g (6 oz) tinned sweetcorn, drained	Scant cup drained canned sweetcorn
Freshly ground black pepper	Freshly ground black pepper
Pinch of dried mixed herbs	Pinch of dried mixed herbs
225 g (½ lb) fresh broccoli florets	½ lb fresh calabrese
150 ml (¼ pint) carrot juice	Generous ½ cup carrot juice
340 g (¾ lb) carrots, peeled and sliced	¾ lb carrots, peeled and sliced
200 g (7 oz) mangetout	7 oz snowpeas
25 g (1 oz) wholemeal breadcrumbs	½ cup wholewheat breadcrumbs
20 g (¾ oz) cheese, grated	Scant ¼ cup shredded cheese

Pre-heat the oven to 190°C/375°F/gas 5.

Clean the potatoes, prick them with a fork, wrap in foil and bake in the pre-heated oven for 50 minutes, or until cooked through.

Meanwhile, place the flaked tuna in a flameproof and oven-proof dish. Add the sweetcorn and season with pepper and herbs. Cover with the broccoli florets and pour the carrot juice over the top. Cover and bake in the oven for 25 minutes.

Cook the carrots in the meantime and make the topping for the bake. To do this, simply mix the wholemeal breadcrumbs with the cheese. Remove the tuna bake from the oven when it has cooked and sprinkle the breadcrumb mixture over the top. Place under a hot grill for 5 minutes. Meanwhile, cook the mangetout.

Serve the Baked Tuna Broccoli with the potatoes, carrots and mangetout.

Turkey Kebabs with Rice and Green Salad

PER SERVING: 399 CALORIES
3 G FAT (⅛ OZ) (7 PER CENT)

SERVES 1

50 g (2 oz) brown rice	¼ cup brown rice
80 g (3 oz) lean turkey, cubed	3 oz lean turkey, cubed
3 cherry tomatoes	3 cherry tomatoes
4 button mushrooms, wiped clean	4 closed mushrooms, wiped clean

¼ yellow pepper, roughly chopped	¼ yellow bell pepper, roughly chopped
1 tbsp lemon juice	1 tbsp lemon juice
Freshly ground black pepper	Freshly ground black pepper
45 g (1½ oz) Chinese leaves, shredded	¼ cup shredded Napa cabbage
2.5-cm (1-in) chunk cucumber, diced	1-in chunk cucumber, diced
2 tsp fat-free French dressing	2 tsp fat-free French dressing

Put the rice on to cook, following the instructions on the pack.

Meanwhile, thread pieces of turkey, tomatoes, mushrooms and pepper alternately on to skewers. Sprinkle with lemon juice and black pepper and grill for a good 10 minutes, turning every few minutes so that all sides are cooked.

Make a salad from the Chinese leaves, cucumber and dressing and serve with the kebabs and rice.

Pork, Apple and Prune Casserole with Sorbet

PER SERVING: 402 CALORIES
10 G (¼ OZ) FAT (22 PER CENT)

SERVES 4

320 g (11 oz) very lean pork, diced	11 oz very lean pork, diced
80 g (3 oz) lean back bacon	3 oz lean Canadian bacon
3 medium apples, chopped	3 medium apples, chopped
8 ready-to-eat prunes	8 ready-to-eat prunes
400 g (14 oz) potatoes, peeled and sliced	14 oz potatoes, peeled and sliced
Salt and freshly ground black pepper	Salt and freshly ground black pepper
450 ml (¾ pint) stock	Scant 2 cups stock
200 g (7 oz) whole baby sweetcorn	7 oz whole baby sweetcorn
240 g (9 oz) sorbet of your choice, such as lemon, blackcurrant or raspberry	9 oz sorbet of your choice, such as lemon, blackcurrant or raspberry

Pre-heat the oven to 180°C/350°F/gas mark 4.

Place the pork in an ovenproof dish. Grill the bacon, then chop and add it to the pork, along with the apples and prunes. Place the potato slices in a layer on top and season to taste. Pour the stock over, adding more if necessary to ensure that it just reaches the top layer of potato. Cover and cook for 55 minutes in the pre-heated oven. Remove the lid and cook for a further 15 minutes until the potatoes have turned golden brown.

Meanwhile, cook the sweetcorn to serve with the casserole.

For dessert, serve 60 g (2½ oz) of sorbet per person.

Skewered Prawns and Monkfish

PER SERVING: 410 CALORIES
10 G (½ OZ) FAT (22 PER CENT)

SERVES 4

2 tbsp olive oil	2 tbsp olive oil
1 tsp chopped fresh thyme	1 tsp chopped fresh thyme
1 tsp chopped fresh dill	1 tsp chopped fresh dill
1 tsp chopped fresh coriander	1 tsp chopped cilantro
Salt and freshly ground black pepper	Salt and freshly ground black pepper
400 g (14 oz) monkfish, washed and cubed	14 oz monkfish, washed and cubed
24 prawns	24 shrimp
280 g (10 oz) tagliatelle	10 oz tagliatelle
100 g (4 oz) young spinach, washed and shredded	4 oz young spinach, washed and shredded

Mix the olive oil with the chopped fresh herbs and add salt and pepper to taste. Thread cubes of the monkfish and prawns alternately on to skewers. Brush with the oil and herb mix and grill for 5 minutes. Turn, brush again and grill for a further 5 minutes. Use up the oil, basting while cooking if necessary.

Meanwhile, cook the tagliatelle according to the instructions on the pack. Drain, mix it with the spinach and spoon it on to four serving plates. Lay the skewers of fish on the tagliatelle and spinach.

Bean Casserole

PER SERVING: 401 CALORIES
3 G (⅛ OZ) FAT (7 PER CENT)

SERVES 4

50 g (2 oz) dried black-eyed beans	¼ cup dried black-eyed beans
50 g (2 oz) dried butter beans	¼ cup dried lima beans
50 g (2 oz) dried haricot beans	¼ cup dried navy beans
50 g (2 oz) dried red kidney beans	Heaped ¼ cup dried red kidney beans
4 tomatoes, chopped	4 tomatoes, chopped
1 green pepper, seeded and chopped	1 green bell pepper, seeded and chopped
50 g (2 oz) mushrooms, wiped and sliced	1 cup wiped, sliced mushrooms
2 tbsp chopped fresh coriander	2 tbsp chopped cilantro
2 cloves	2 cloves
2 tbsp clear honey	2 tbsp clear honey
1 tbsp wine vinegar	1 tbsp wine vinegar
Salt and freshly ground black pepper	Salt and freshly ground black pepper
240 g (9 oz) brown rice	1¼ cups brown rice

Soak all the beans, except the red kidney beans, in plenty of water overnight. Soak the red kidney beans in a separate bowl, also overnight.

Next day, drain the red kidney beans, change the water and boil rapidly for a full 10 minutes. Drain and rinse all the beans, then cook all of them together for 1 hour in fresh water until tender.

Then stir in the tomatoes, green pepper, mushrooms,

coriander and cloves. Add the honey and wine vinegar and season to taste with salt and pepper. Simmer for a further 30 minutes. Meanwhile, cook the rice, then serve with the casserole.

The Low-fat Diet

In this diet, the meals have been planned in such a way that just 30 per cent of their calories come from fat. If you prefer to have a cooked meal at lunchtime and a lighter meal in the evening, just swap the lunches and dinners around.

If you are trying to lose weight rather than just protect your gallbladder, you can cut out the snacks, stick to just 300 ml (½ pint/1¼ cups) of skimmed milk and have two of the lunches each day as your two meals – these have 100 fewer calories than the dinners. To shave off another 100 calories, you could choose breakfasts from the Reducing Diet that follows, which would bring the total to 1,400.

The total calories per day have been divided as follows:

- breakfasts, 400
- lunches, 500
- dinners, 600

plus:

- 600 ml (1 pint/2½ cups) skimmed milk, 200
- snacks, 200.

Low-fat Snacks to Have Anytime (each around 100 calories)

99 calories
0.3 g fat
   Low-fat potato waffles.
97 calories
1.5 g fat
   35-g (1½-oz) slice Swiss roll (jelly roll).
91 calories
0.0 g fat
   8 g (¼ oz) dried apricots.
90 calories
3.0 g fat
   45-g (1½-oz) slice Arctic roll (ice-cream jelly roll).
91 calories
0.0 g fat
   150-g (5-oz) portion jelly (jello).
92 calories
0.2 g fat
   100-g (4-oz) portion low-fat rice pudding.
84 calories
1.2 g fat
   Small pot of plain yogurt.
87 calories
0.0 g fat
   Ice lolly.
50–100 calories
0.0 g fat
   Piece of fruit.
94 calories
2.0 g fat
   2 Jaffa cakes.

80 calories
1.8 g fat
    2 garibaldi biscuits.
104 calories
2.2 g fat
    2 fig rolls.
70 calories
2.2 g fat
    2 rich tea biscuits.
100 calories
1.1 g fat
    1 finger roll.
90 calories
1.3 g fat
    Lemon and raisin pancake.
80 calories
0.4 g fat
    Crumpet (English muffin).

Breakfasts

Weetabix, Banana and Toasted Sesame Seeds

404 CALORIES

3 G (⅛ OZ) FAT (7 PER CENT)

2 Weetabix	2 Weetabix
1 large banana, chopped	1 large banana, chopped
½ tsp sesame seeds, toasted	½ tsp sesame seeds, toasted
200 ml (⅓ pint) skimmed milk	Scant cup skim milk

Serve the Weetabix with the chopped banana on top. Sprinkle
with the sesame seeds and pour the milk over the top.

Grilled Tomatoes on Toast with Baked Beans

401 CALORIES
8 G (¼ OZ) FAT (17 PER CENT)

2 slices wholemeal bread	2 slices wholewheat bread
2 tsp low-fat spread	2 tsp low-fat spread
100 g (4 oz) baked beans	1½ cups baked beans
2 tomatoes, halved	2 tomatoes, halved
175 ml (6 fl oz) grapefruit juice, chilled	⅔ cup grapefruit juice, chilled

Toast the bread and spread with the low-fat spread. Heat the beans and spoon on to the toast. Grill the tomato halves and serve with the beans on toast. Have the grapefruit juice with it.

Instant Oat Cereal with Apple and Toast and Honey

395 CALORIES
7 G (⅛ OZ) FAT (16 PER CENT)

45 g (1½ oz) instant porridge	½ cup instant oatmeal
175 ml (6 fl oz) skimmed milk	⅔ cup skim milk
2 tbsp sweetened stewed apple	2 tbsp applesauce
1 tsp raisins	1 tsp raisins
1 slice wholemeal bread	1 slice wholewheat bread
1 tsp low-fat spread	1 tsp low-fat spread
1 tsp honey	1 tsp honey

Make up the cereal, warming the milk, as directed on the pack. Serve with the apple and raisins. Toast the bread and serve with the low-fat spread and honey.

Winter Fruits with Yogurt and Crunchy Muesli

396 CALORIES
4 G (⅛ OZ) FAT (8 PER CENT)

3 ready-to-eat apricots	3 ready-to-eat apricots
3 ready-to-eat prunes	3 ready-to-eat prunes
3 ready-to-eat apple slices	3 ready-to-eat apple slices
55 ml (2 fl oz) fresh orange juice	¼ cup fresh orange juice
Small pot low-fat plain yogurt	Small pot low-fat plain yogurt
2 tbsp crunchy muesli	2 tbsp granola
100 ml (3½ fl oz) skimmed milk	Scant ½ cup skim milk

Soak the fruits in the orange juice, plus a little extra water to cover if necessary, overnight.

In the morning, spoon the yogurt over the top and sprinkle on the crunchy muesli. Serve with the skimmed milk.

Grapefruit and Orange Bowl with Granary Toast and Jam

397 CALORIES
9 G (¼ OZ) FAT (12 PER CENT)

½ a grapefruit, divided into segments	½ a grapefruit, divided into segments
1 orange, divided into segments	1 orange, divided into segments
2 slices Granary bread	2 slices graham bread
1 tsp low-fat spread	1 tsp low-fat spread
2 tsp jam of your choice	2 tsp jelly of your choice

Mix the grapefruit and orange segments together in a bowl and chill before serving.

Meanwhile, toast the bread and top with the low-fat spread and jam. Serve with the chilled grapefruit and orange.

Toasted Bagels with Cream Cheese and Peaches and Orange Juice

402 CALORIES
13 G (½ OZ) FAT (29 PER CENT)

1 bagel	1 bagel
1 tbsp cream cheese	1 tbsp cream cheese
1 peach, sliced	1 peach, sliced
200 ml (⅓ pint) orange juice	Scant cup orange juice

Slice the bagel in half and toast. Spread with the cream cheese and top with the slices of peach. Serve with a glass of orange juice.

Pineapple Smoothie and Wholegrain Toast

398 CALORIES
6 G (⅛ OZ) FAT (13 PER CENT)

100 g (4 oz) fresh or tinned pineapple	½ cup fresh or canned pineapple
1 large banana	1 large banana
Small pot plain low-fat yogurt	Small pot plain low-fat yogurt
2 tbsp crushed ice	2 tbsp crushed ice
1 slice wholemeal bread	1 slice wholewheat bread
1 tsp low-fat spread	1 tsp low-fat spread

Blend together the pineapple, banana and yogurt, then add the crushed ice.

Toast the bread and spread with the low-fat spread.

Lunches (each around 400 calories)

Baked Potato with Cottage Cheese and Chives

502 CALORIES
13 G (½ OZ) FAT (24 PER CENT)

180-g (6-oz) baking potato	6-oz baking potato
110 g (4 oz) cottage cheese	½ cup cottage cheese
Handful fresh chives, chopped	Handful fresh chives, chopped
1 tomato, chopped	1 tomato, chopped

Pre-heat the oven to 190°C/375°F/gas 5.

Wash the potato, prick it with a fork and bake in the pre-heated oven for 50 minutes, or until it is cooked.

Meanwhile, mix the remaining ingredients together. Split the potato and spoon the cottage cheese mix into it.

Butter Bean Bap with Orange Juice and a Nectarine

502 CALORIES
9 G (¼ OZ) FAT (16 PER CENT)

60 g (2½ oz) tinned butter beans, drained	Heaped 1½ cups drained canned lima beans
1 tsp olive oil	1 tsp olive oil
Pinch dried mustard	Pinch dried mustard
Freshly ground black pepper	Freshly ground black pepper
1 large Granary bap	1 large graham roll
1 pineapple ring	1 pineapple ring
Mustard and cress	Mustard and cress
150 ml (¼ pint) orange juice	Generous ½ cup orange juice
1 nectarine	1 nectarine

Mash the butter beans with the olive oil, mustard and black pepper to taste. Split the bap and spread the bean puree over the lower half. Top with the pineapple ring and sprinkle the mustard and cress over it. Replace the top half of the bap.

Serve with the orange juice in a tall glass and finish the meal with the nectarine.

Savoury Scone with Coleslaw and a Pear

495 CALORIES
16 G (½ OZ) FAT (29 PER CENT)

90 g (3½ oz) white cabbage, shredded	Scant cup shredded white cabbage
1 carrot, grated	1 carrot, shredded
1 apple, grated	1 apple, shredded
2 tbsp reduced-fat salad cream or mayonnaise	2 tbsp reduced-fat salad cream or mayonnaise
1 tbsp raisins	1 tbsp raisins
1 savoury scone	1 savoury biscuit
1 pear	1 pear

Make up some coleslaw by mixing the cabbage with the carrot, apple and salad cream or mayonnaise. Mix in the raisins. Serve the coleslaw with the savoury scone and have the pear for dessert.

Salmon with Beans and Raspberries

495 CALORIES
11 G (¼ OZ) FAT (20 PER CENT)

60 g (2½ oz) tinned salmon, drained	Generous ⅛ cup drained canned salmon
60 g (2½ oz) tinned cannellini beans, drained	½ cup canned drained cannellini beans
50 g (2 oz) tinned broad beans, drained	⅓ cup drained canned fava beans

2 tsp oil-free French dressing	2 tsp oil-free French dressing
1 tbsp chopped fresh flat-leaf parsley	1 tbsp chopped fresh flat-leaf parsley
120-g (4½-oz) chunk French bread	4½-oz chunk French bread
60 g (2½ oz) raspberries or other fresh fruit	½ cup raspberries or other fresh fruit

Mix together the fish and beans. Pour over the dressing and sprinkle the parsley over the top. Serve with the French bread.

Serve the fruit for dessert.

Ham Ploughmans and Tomato Juice

499 CALORIES
11 G FAT (21 PER CENT)

1 tsp low-fat spread	1 tsp low-fat spread
2 thick slices wholemeal bread	2 thick slices wholewheat bread
80 g (3 oz) ham	3 oz ham
2 large pickled onions	2 large pickled onions
1 apple	1 apple
1 tbsp sweet pickle	1 tbsp relish
1–2 lettuce leaves, washed	1–2 lettuce leaves, washed
200 ml (⅓ pint) tomato juice	Scant cup tomato juice
Dash of Worcestershire sauce	Dash of Worcestershire sauce
1–2 drops Tabasco sauce	1–2 drops hot pepper sauce

Spread the low-fat spread on the bread and then arrange all but the last three ingredients on a plate. To the tomato juice add each of the sauces to taste and serve with the ploughmans.

Ciabatta Pizza and an Orange

406 CALORIES
10 G (¼ OZ) FAT (21 PER CENT)

¼ small aubergine, sliced

½ small red pepper, chopped

60-g (2½-oz) piece ciabatta bread

2 tbsp tomato purée

1 tomato, sliced

1 rasher lean back bacon, chopped

15 g (½ oz) reduced-fat Cheddar, grated

2 sprigs of fresh basil, to garnish

1 orange

¼ small eggplant, sliced

½ small red bell pepper, chopped

2½-oz piece ciabatta bread

2 tbsp tomato paste

1 tomato, sliced

1 slice lean Canadian bacon, chopped

Scant ¼ cup shredded reduced-fat Cheddar

2 sprigs of fresh basil, to garnish

1 orange

Grill the aubergine and peppers gently for about 5 minutes each side.

Meanwhile, split the ciabatta lengthways and spread each cut side with half the tomato puree. Lay the slices of tomato and chopped pieces of bacon on top and add the aubergine and red pepper when they are ready. Sprinkle the grated cheese over the top. Grill for 8 minutes and serve garnished with the basil. Have the orange for dessert.

Mini Pitta with Hummus and Fruit Salad

492 CALORIES
11 G (¼ OZ) FAT (21 PER CENT)

1 mini pitta bread	1 mini pitta bread
55 g (2 oz) hummus	4 tbsp hummus
1 small apple	1 small apple
1 small pear	1 small pear
1 small banana	1 small banana
60 g (2½ oz) plain low-fat fromage frais	¼ cup plain low-fat fromage blanc

Warm the pitta and cut it into strips. Serve with the hummus as a dip.

Chop up the apple, pear and banana and mix together with the fromage frais for dessert.

Dinners (each around 600 calories)

Tandoori Chicken and Lemon and Orange Sorbet

PER SERVING: 601 CALORIES
10 G (¼ OZ) FAT (16 PER CENT)

SERVES 4

4 x 120-g (4½-oz) chicken breasts	4 x 4½-oz chicken breasts
300 g (11 oz) plain low-fat yogurt	300 g (11 oz) plain low-fat yogurt
1 tbsp olive oil	1 tbsp olive oil

1 tsp ground ginger
1 tsp chilli powder
1 tsp paprika
2 cloves garlic, crushed
2 tbsp tomato purée
240 g (9 oz) brown rice
Lemon slices and a few sprigs
of chopped, fresh parsley,
to garnish
400 g (14 oz) lemon sorbet
2 oranges, peeled and cut into
segments

1 tsp ground ginger
1 tsp chili powder
1 tsp paprika
2 cloves garlic, crushed
2 tbsp tomato paste
1¼ cups brown rice
Lemon slices and a few sprigs of
fresh parsley, chopped,
to garnish
14 oz lemon sorbet
2 oranges, peeled and cut into
segments

Remove the skin from the chicken breasts. Mix together the yogurt, olive oil, ginger, chilli powder, paprika, garlic and tomato purée. Coat the chicken with the mixture and leave, covered, in the fridge to marinate for 10 hours.

When ready to cook, grill each side for 15 minutes.

Meanwhile, cook the brown rice, drain and stir in some of the parsley. Garnish with the lemon and remaining parsley.

For dessert, have the sorbet topped with the orange segments.

Rigatoni with Yellow Pepper and Tomato Sauce and Strawberries with Cointreau

PER SERVING: 605 CALORIES
12 G (¼ OZ) FAT (18 PER CENT)

SERVES 4

1 tbsp olive oil	1 tbsp olive oil
260 g (9 oz) aubergine, thickly sliced	9 oz eggplant, thickly sliced
1 yellow pepper, seeded and sliced	1 yellow bell pepper, seeded and sliced
1 clove garlic, crushed	1 clove garlic, minced
Salt and freshly ground black pepper	Salt and freshly ground black pepper
360 g (¾ lb) tomatoes, chopped	¾ lb tomatoes, chopped
12 fresh basil leaves	12 fresh basil leaves
Sprig of fresh thyme	Sprig of fresh thyme
400 g (14 oz) rigatoni	14 oz rigatoni
36 black olives	36 black olives
15 g (½ oz) Parmesan cheese, finely grated	Heaped tbsp finely shredded Parmesan cheese
1 medium crisp lettuce, washed	1 medium crisp lettuce, washed
½ cucumber, diced	½ cucumber, diced
200 g (7 oz) strawberries, hulled, washed and halved	7 oz strawberries, hulled, washed and halved
2 tbsp Cointreau	2 tbsp Cointreau
150 g (5 oz) orange-flavoured yogurt	1½ cups orange-flavoured yogurt
60 g (2½ oz) quark	Generous ½ cup ricotta

Heat the oil and fry the aubergine slices gently for a few minutes, then add the yellow pepper and garlic. Season to taste, cover and simmer for 10 minutes.

Add the tomatoes, basil and thyme and cook for a further 15 minutes.

Meanwhile, cook the rigatoni according to the instructions on the pack. Drain well. Spoon on to four serving plates, top with the aubergine and sauce, then sprinkle the olives and Parmesan cheese over the top. Arrange the lettuce and cucumber on side plates and serve with the dish.

For dessert, divide the strawberries among four bowls. Stir the Cointreau into the yogurt, then mix in the quark. Serve this creamy mixture in spoonfuls with the strawberries.

Ruby Grapefruit and Tarragon Sole with Baked Apple and Custard

PER SERVING: 600 CALORIES

8 G (¼ OZ) FAT (12 PER CENT)

SERVES 4

4 x 100-g (4-oz) lemon sole fillets, skinned	4 x 4-oz sole fillets, skinned
Zest of ½ a grapefruit	Zest of ½ a grapefruit
½ grapefruit	½ grapefruit
150 g (5 oz) cottage cheese	Generous ½ cup cottage cheese
4 spring onions, roughly chopped	4 scallions, roughly chopped
2 tsp chopped fresh tarragon	2 tsp chopped fresh tarragon

Salt and freshly ground black pepper	Salt and freshly ground black pepper
750 g (1½ lb) potatoes, peeled	1½ lb potatoes, peeled
2 tbsp cornflour	2 tbsp cornstarch
200 g (7 oz) mangetout	7 oz snowpeas
4 large baking apples	4 large tart apples
40 g (1½ oz) demerara sugar	¼ cup coarse light brown sugar
20 g (¾ oz) raisins	1 tbsp raisins
30 g (1 oz) almonds, toasted	¼ cup almonds, toasted
Pinch of mixed spice	Pinch of mixed spice
600 ml (1 pint) ready-to-serve low-fat custard	2½ cups ready-to-serve low-fat custard

Place the fillets in a pan with the grapefruit zest. Cover with water and simmer for about 7 minutes until tender.

While the fish is cooking, cut the grapefruit segments from the pith. Place the cottage cheese, spring onions, tarragon, salt and pepper in a blender and blend until smooth.

When it is ready, transfer the fish, reserving the cooking juices, to a heatproof dish and keep warm.

Boil the potatoes until tender. Blend 175 ml (6 fl oz/¾ cup) of the reserved juices with the cornflour. Stir in a pan over a medium heat until the mixture thickens into a sauce. Also, cook the mangetout. Arrange a fillet of sole on each of four serving plates and pour the sauce over. Serve the potatoes and mangetout.

To make the dessert, pre-heat the oven to 180°C/350°F/gas 4. Core the baking apples, cut a quarter of the core off the bottom of each one and use these as stoppers in the bottoms of the apples to stop the filling running out. Run a sharp knife round the middle of all the skins. Fill the centres with a mix of the sugar, raisins, almonds and mixed spice. Place in a baking dish with 3 tablespoons of water and and bake in the pre-heated oven for 45 minutes to 1 hour, until they are soft all the way through. Heat up the custard and serve with the apples.

Lamb with Raspberry Sauce and Rice Pudding

PER SERVING: 604 CALORIES
22 G (¾ OZ) FAT (33 PER CENT)

SERVES 4

4 x 90-g (3½-oz) extra lean lamb fillets	4 x 3½-oz extra lean lamb fillets
600 g (1¼ lb) potatoes	1¼ lb potatoes
Knob of margarine or butter	Pat of margarine or butter
100 ml (3½ fl oz) skimmed milk	½ cup skim milk
Salt and freshly ground black pepper	Salt and freshly ground black pepper
300 g (11 oz) tinned raspberries in syrup	2¼ cups canned raspberries in syrup
Large sprig of rosemary	Large sprig of rosemary
1 tsp dried rosemary, ground	1 tsp dried rosemary, ground
2 tsp cornflour	2 tsp cornstarch
600 g (1¼ lb) tinned low-fat rice pudding or home-made with skimmed milk	1¼ lb canned low-fat rice pudding or home-made with skim milk
12 tinned prunes	12 canned prunes

Grill the lamb fillets for 8 minutes on each side. Peel, chop and boil the potatoes, drain and mash with the margarine or butter and milk and season well.

Heat the raspberries with their syrup together with the rosemary and ground rosemary. Mix the cornflour with a little water in a cup and add to the raspberries. Stir over a medium heat until the syrup has thickened and pour over the grilled lamb. Serve with the mashed potatoes.

For dessert, heat the rice pudding and serve with 3 prunes each.

Oven-baked Mackerel-stuffed Mushrooms and Banana Split

PER SERVING: 590 CALORIES

15 G (½ OZ) FAT (23 PER CENT)

SERVES 4

4 large flat mushrooms	4 large flat mushrooms
185 g (6½ oz) tinned mackerel in mustard sauce	6½ oz canned mackerel in mustard sauce
½ tsp curry powder	½ tsp curry powder
Salt and freshly ground black pepper	Salt and freshly ground black pepper
2 spring onions, chopped	2 scallions, chopped
2 tbsp chopped fresh parsley	2 tbsp chopped fresh parsley
4 x 120-g (4½-oz) chunks French stick	4 x 4½-oz chunks French stick
4 bananas	4 bananas
240 g (9 oz) reduced-calorie raspberry ripple ice-cream	9 oz reduced-calorie raspberry ripple ice-cream

Pre-heat the oven to 180°C/350°F/gas 4.

Wipe the mushrooms, cut off the stalks and chop them. Place the mushroom caps dark side up on a large piece of foil. Mix the mackerel with the mushroom stalks and curry powder and season to taste. Add the spring onions and half the fresh parsley. Pile the mixture into the mushroom caps. If there is any left, just pile it on the foil to the side. Pull the foil up to encase the stuffed mushrooms and bake in the pre-heated oven for 30 minutes.

Heat the bread. Sprinkle the remaining parsley over the mushrooms before serving with the bread.

For dessert, serve each person with a banana, split lengthways, with 60 g (2½ oz) each of ice-cream spread between the two halves.

Bean Burgers

PER SERVING: 600 CALORIES
11 G (¼ OZ) FAT (17 PER CENT)

SERVES 4

75 g (3 oz) dried chickpeas	Scant ½ cup dried garbanzos
2 carrots	2 carrots
2 onions	2 onions
1 green pepper	1 green bell pepper
2 celery sticks	2 celery sticks
1 tsp dried mixed herbs	1 tsp dried mixed herbs
Salt and freshly ground black pepper	Salt and freshly ground black pepper
1 egg, beaten	1 egg, beaten

4 burger buns	4 burger buns
4 lettuce leaves, washed	4 lettuce leaves, washed
2 tomatoes, sliced	2 tomatoes, sliced
4 tsp chutney	4 tsp chutney
4 x 100-g (4-oz) individual crème caramels	4 x 4-oz individual crème caramels
4 peaches	4 peaches
4 plain biscuits	4 plain cookies

Soak the chickpeas overnight in a bowl of water.

The next day, drain the chickpeas, put them in a pan, cover with water, bring to the boil and simmer for 1 hour, checking from time to time that there is still enough water.

Meanwhile, finely chop then steam the carrots, onions, green pepper and celery. Once they are soft, stir in the mixed herbs and season to taste. Blend the chickpeas and vegetables so that they are well mixed, but the texture should still be coarse. Mix in the beaten egg to bind, then make into 4 burgers. Grill them for 10 minutes on each side. Split open the burger buns and grill the inside sides of each lightly. Place the cooked bean burgers on the lower halves of the buns, top with a layer of lettuce, tomato and chutney and then the top half of the bun.

Have a 100-g (4-oz) portion of crème caramel per person for dessert, served with a sliced peach each on the side and a plain biscuit, for added crunch.

Stir-fried Chilli Pork

PER SERVING: 600 CALORIES
15 G (¼ OZ) FAT (22 PER CENT)

SERVES 4

450 g (1 lb) extra lean pork	1 lb extra lean pork
10 g (¼ oz) muscovado sugar	1 tbsp dark brown sugar
1 clove of garlic, crushed	1 clove of garlic, minced
Pinch of five spice powder	Pinch of five spice powder
½ tsp ground cumin	½ tsp ground cumin
240 g (9 oz) brown rice	1¼ cups brown rice
175 g (6 oz) broccoli	6 oz calabrese
2 tbsp olive oil	2 tbsp olive oil
1 yellow pepper, seeded and chopped	1 yellow bell pepper, seeded and chopped
100 g (4 oz) mushrooms, wiped and chopped	2 cups wiped and chopped mushrooms
1 onion, sliced	1 onion, sliced
1 tbsp water	1 tbsp water
100 g (4 oz) tinned water chestnuts, drained	4 oz canned water chestnuts,
Dash of soy sauce	Dash of soy sauce
Handful chives, chopped	Handful chives, chopped

Cut the pork into thin slices. Mix the muscovado sugar with the garlic, a good pinch of five spice powder and the cumin. Put the sugar mixture in a dish with the pork and mix well. Leave for 30 minutes.

Meanwhile, cook the brown rice according to the instructions on the pack. While it is cooking, prepare the broccoli by breaking it into small florets and blanch them for 1 minute in boiling water.

When the pork is ready, heat the oil in a wok or heavy based frying pan. When the oil is hot, add the pork and fry for 4 minutes. Add the broccoli, pepper, mushrooms, onion, water and water chestnuts. Add a dash of soy sauce to taste, cover and simmer for a further minute. Sprinkle the chives over and serve with the rice.

The Reducing Diet

This diet has been designed to help those wanting to shed some excess weight to do so carefully and gradually without compromising the overall nutritional quality of their diet. The day's calories have been divided up as follows:

- breakfast, 300
- lunches, 400
- dinners, 400

making a total of 1,100, plus the following extras:

- 300 ml (½ pint/1¼ cups) skimmed milk, 100
- piece of fruit of your choice, 100

making 1,300 calories daily altogether.

Breakfasts (around 300 calories)

Fresh Figs with Fromage Frais and Wholemeal Toast

304 CALORIES
4 G (⅛ OZ) FAT (11 PER CENT)

2 fresh figs	2 fresh figs
3 tbsp low-fat fromage frais	3 tbsp low-fat fromage blanc
1 slice wholemeal toast	1 slice wholewheat toast
1 tsp low-fat spread	1 tsp low-fat spread

Peel the figs and cut them into quarters. Serve with the low-fat fromage frais. Have the slice of wholemeal toast with it, spread with the low-fat spread.

Bacon Sandwich

295 CALORIES
4 G (⅛ OZ) FAT (12 PER CENT)

2 slices wholemeal bread	2 slices wholewheat bread
2 tsp low-fat spread	2 tsp low-fat spread
1 rasher lean back bacon	1 slice lean Canadian bacon
1 tomato, sliced	1 tomato, sliced
Freshly ground black pepper	Freshly ground black pepper

Spread one slice of the wholemeal bread with spread. Grill the bacon, chop it into pieces and place on top. Cover with slices of tomato. Grind over some fresh black pepper. Top with the second slice of bread and serve.

Melon and Grapefruit Salad and Toast with Marmalade

290 CALORIES
5 G (⅛ OZ) FAT (16 PER CENT)

½ grapefruit	½ grapefruit
2 large slices of melon	2 large slices of melon
2 slices wholemeal bread	2 slices wholewheat bread
1 tsp low-fat spread	1 tsp low-fat spread
2 tsp marmalade	2 tsp marmalade

Cut the grapefruit into segments and serve on a plate with the melon slices. Follow with the wholemeal bread, fresh or toasted, and served with spread and marmalade.

Poached Egg on Granary Bread and Orange Juice

290 CALORIES
9 G (¼ OZ) FAT (29 PER CENT)

1 egg	1 egg
3 mushrooms	3 mushrooms
1 thick slice Granary bread	1 thick slice graham bread
1 tsp low-fat spread	1 tsp low-fat spread

| 200 ml (⅓ pint) orange or other fruit juice | Scant cup orange or other fruit juice |

Poach the egg and grill the mushrooms. Toast the Granary bread, spread with the low-fat spread and serve with the egg and mushrooms.

Pour the orange juice or other juice of your choice into a tall glass to have with your breakfast.

Smoked Salmon on Rye with Fresh Grapefruit

302 CALORIES
4 G (⅛ OZ) FAT (11 PER CENT)

½ grapefruit	½ grapefruit
2 tsp brown sugar	2 tsp brown sugar
2 tsp cream cheese	2 tsp cream cheese
2 rye crispbreads	2 rye crackers
56 g (2 oz) smoked salmon	2 oz smoked salmon

Prepare the grapefruit by carefully working a small, sharp knife between the segments and the skin, separating them. Sprinkle the sugar over the top.

Spread the cheese on the crispbreads and put equal amounts of the salmon on each, laying it on top of the cheese.

Peanut Butter and Toast with Orange Juice

291 CALORIES
7 G (¼ OZ) FAT (23 PER CENT)

2 slices wholemeal bread
2 tsp peanut butter
200 ml (⅓ pint) orange or other fruit or vegetable juice

2 slices wholemeal bread
2 tsp peanut butter
Scant cup orange or other fruit or vegetable juice

Toast the bread and spread the peanut butter on them.

Serve with the glass of orange or other fruit or vegetable juice of your choice.

Croissant with Jam and Fruit Juice

293 CALORIES
10 G (¼ OZ) FAT (32 PER CENT)

1 croissant
2 tsp jam
225 ml (⅓ pint) ruby red grapefruit juice

1 croissant
2 tsp jelly
Scant cup ruby red grapefruit juice

Heat the croissant and serve with the jam.

Pour the grapefruit juice into a glass to accompany it.

Lunches (each about 400 calories)

Gazpacho with Granary Bread and a Fresh Peach

401 CALORIES
4 G (⅛ OZ) FAT (8 PER CENT)

400 ml (14 fl oz) tomato juice, chilled	1¾ cups tomato juice, chilled
1 clove garlic, crushed	1 clove garlic, minced
3 tbsp wine vinegar	3 tbsp wine vinegar
2 tbsp chopped fresh basil	2 tbsp chopped fresh basil
Pinch of celery salt	Pinch of celery salt
1 green pepper, seeded and chopped	1 green pepper, seeded and chopped
½ cucumber, chopped	½ cucumber, chopped
1 celery stick	1 celery stick
Salt and freshly ground black pepper	Salt and freshly ground black pepper
1 large slice Granary bread	1 large slice graham bread
1 peach	1 peach

Blend the tomato juice with the garlic and vinegar. Add the basil, celery salt, green pepper, cucumber and celery. Blend again. Season and chill.

Serve with the bread and follow with a juicy peach for dessert.

Baked Potato with Ham and Mushrooms and a Kiwi Fruit

401 CALORIES
4 G (⅛ OZ) FAT (9 PER CENT)

1 medium baking potato	1 medium baking potato
60 g (2½ oz) fromage frais	Generous ¼ cup fromage blanc
60 g (2½ oz) lean ham, chopped	2½ oz lean ham, chopped
2 mushrooms, chopped	2 mushrooms, chopped
2 tsp chopped fresh parsley	2 tsp chopped fresh parsley
Salt	Salt
1 tbsp sweet pickle	1 tbsp relish
1 kiwi fruit	1 kiwi fruit

Pre-heat the oven to 190°C/375°F/gas 5.

Scrub the potato and prick it with a fork. Bake it in the pre-heated oven for 45 minutes or until tender.

Once it is cooked, cut the potato in half lengthways and scoop out the soft insides. Mix this with the fromage frais, ham, mushrooms and parsley and season with salt to taste. Pile the potato mixture back into the potato skins and serve with sweet pickle.

Have the kiwi fruit for dessert.

Peasant Chicken Salad and an Apple

390 CALORIES
7 G (⅛ OZ) FAT (17 PER CENT)

150 g (5 oz) brown macaroni	Generous cup brown macaroni
80 g (3 oz) cooked lean chicken, chopped	3 oz cooked lean chicken, chopped
Juice of 1 lemon	Juice of 1 lemon
1 tsp chopped fresh basil	1 tsp chopped fresh basil
1 carrot, grated	1 carrot, shredded
1 tbsp reduced-fat salad cream or mayonnaise	1 tbsp reduced-fat salad cream or mayonnaise
1 apple	1 apple

Cook the macaroni according to the instructions on the pack.

Meanwhile, mix the chicken with the lemon juice, basil, carrot and salad cream or mayonnaise. Drain the macaroni and chill it and the chicken mixture.

Mix the macaroni and chicken mixture together before serving, and have the apple for dessert.

Fruit, Nut and Rice Pot

393 CALORIES
8 G (¼ OZ) FAT (19 PER CENT)

130 g (4¾ oz) cooked brown rice	Generous ⅔ cup cooked brown rice
1 tbsp chopped hazelnuts	1 tbsp chopped hazelnuts
1 slice pineapple, chopped	1 slice pineapple, chopped
1 small banana, sliced	1 small banana, sliced
10 g raisins	1 tbsp raisins
2 tsp chopped fresh basil	2 tsp chopped fresh basil
Salt and freshly ground black pepper	Salt and freshly ground black pepper

In a bowl, combine all the ingredients, season to taste, then serve.

Roast Beef and Horseradish Sandwich with a Pear

404 CALORIES
8 G (¼ OZ) FAT (17 PER CENT)

2 thick slices wholemeal bread	2 thick slices wholewheat bread
1 tsp low-fat spread	1 tsp low-fat spread
45-g (1½-oz) slice lean beef	1½-oz slice lean beef
1 tsp horseradish sauce	1 tsp horseradish sauce
2 lettuce leaves, washed	2 lettuce leaves, washed
4 slices cucumber	4 slices cucumber
1 pear	1 pear

Spread the low-fat spread on the bread. Top one slice with the beef and spread a little horseradish sauce over it to taste. Follow with the lettuce and slices of cucumber. Complete the sandwich by laying the remaining piece of bread over the top.

Serve the pear for dessert.

Potato, Walnut and Apple Salad

394 CALORIES
16 G (½ OZ) FAT (36 PER CENT)

100 g (4 oz) new potatoes, scrubbed

20 g (¾ oz) walnuts, chopped

6 or so leaves of mint, finely sliced

1 apple, diced

1 tsp lemon juice

2 tbsp low-fat yogurt

Freshly ground black pepper

4 oz new potatoes, scrubbed

¼ cup chopped walnuts

6 or so leaves of mint, finely sliced

1 apple, diced

1 tsp lemon juice

2 tbsp low-fat yogurt

Freshly ground black pepper

Boil, drain and cool the potatoes.

When the potatoes are ready, dice them and add the walnuts and mint. Toss the apple in the lemon juice, then add to the potatoes. Spoon the yogurt over the salad and grind over black pepper to taste. You can then either serve the salad immediately or chill it before eating.

Turkey Kebab

396 CALORIES
9 G (¼ OZ) FAT (4 PER CENT)

90 g (3½ oz) lean turkey, cubed	3½ oz lean turkey, cubed
1 tsp olive oil	1 tsp olive oil
Freshly ground black pepper	Freshly ground black pepper
Pinch of dried mixed herbs	Pinch of dried mixed herbs
1 pitta bread	1 pitta bread
50 g (2 oz) cabbage, shredded	½ cup shredded cabbage
1 carrot, grated	1 carrot, shredded
¼ onion, sliced	¼ onion, sliced
1 tomato, chopped	1 tomato, chopped
Juice of 1 lemon	Juice of 1 lemon

Thread the cubes of turkey on to a large skewer. Mix the oil with pepper to taste and the herbs. Brush this mixture lightly over the turkey. Grill for 15 minutes, turning regularly, until well cooked.

Meanwhile, split the pitta bread along one edge. Mix the cabbage, carrot, onion and tomato and use the mixture to fill the pitta. Lay the turkey kebab on the salad filling and remove the skewer. Drizzle the lemon juice over the turkey and salad and serve.

Dinners (each around 400 calories)

Pork and Boston Beans

PER SERVING: 401 CALORIES
10 G (¼ OZ) FAT (22 PER CENT)

SERVES 2

240 g (9 oz) potatoes, peeled and roughly chopped
150-g (5-oz) lean pork fillet
1 tsp low-fat spread
100 ml (3½ fl oz) skimmed milk
Salt and freshly ground black pepper
150 g (5 oz) baked beans
150 g (5 oz) tinned red kidney beans
Dash of Worcestershire sauce
Pinch of mustard powder

1½ cups peeled and roughly chopped potatoes
5-oz lean pork fillet
1 tsp low-fat spread
Scant ½ cup skim milk
Salt and freshly ground black pepper
1 cup baked beans
1 cup drained canned red kidney beans
Dash of Worcestershire sauce
Pinch of mustard powder

Boil the potatoes.

Meanwhile, grill the pork fillets under a hot grill for around 8 minutes each side.

Drain the potatoes, add the low-fat spread and milk, season to taste, and mash.

Also, stir together the two types of beans, add the Worcestershire sauce and mustard powder and heat through. Put the pork fillets on to plates, pour the beans over and serve with the mashed potato.

Vegetable Couscous with Strawberries and Raspberries with Greek Yoghurt

PER SERVING: 397 CALORIES
11 G (¼ OZ) FAT (25 PER CENT)

SERVES 2

2 tbsp olive oil	2 tbsp olive oil
1 onion, chopped	1 onion, chopped
1 clove garlic, crushed	1 clove garlic, minced
1 tsp tomato purée	1 tsp tomato paste
Salt and freshly ground black pepper	Salt and freshly ground black pepper
Pinch of cumin	Pinch of cumin
Pinch of turmeric	Pinch of turmeric
Pinch of paprika	Pinch of paprika
Pinch of ground coriander	Pinch of ground coriander
Pinch of ground ginger	Pinch of ground ginger
1 tsp chilli sauce	1 tsp chili sauce
300 ml (½ pint) water	1¼ cups water
1 carrot, sliced	1 carrot, sliced
1 potato, diced	1 potato, diced
55 g (2 oz) turnip, diced	⅓ cup diced turnip
1 tomato, chopped	1 tomato, chopped
1 courgette, sliced	1 zucchini, sliced
200 g (7 oz) tinned chickpeas, drained	1½ cups drained canned garbanzos
100 g (4 oz) instant couscous	⅔ cup instant couscous
60 g (2½ oz) raspberries	½ cup raspberries
100 g (4 oz) strawberries, hulled, washed and halved	Scant cup strawberries, hulled, washed and halved
4 tbsp Greek yogurt	4 tbsp Greek yogurt

Heat the oil in a large pan and add the onion and garlic. Cook for a few minutes, stirring well until softened. Add the tomato purée, a pinch each of salt and pepper, the cumin, turmeric, paprika, coriander, ginger and chilli sauce. Pour in half the water, cover, bring to the boil and simmer for 15 minutes.

Add the carrot, potato and turnip. Cover and cook for a further 30 minutes.

Add the tomato, courgette, and chickpeas. Adjust the seasoning to taste if necessary and cook for 15 minutes more.

Meanwhile, make up the couscous according to the instructions on the pack. Serve with the vegetables.

For dessert, serve the raspberries and strawberries mixed together, each portion topped with a spoonful of Greek yogurt.

Smoked Cod Pie with Blackberry Meringue Cases

PER SERVING: 395 CALORIES
2 G FAT (5 PER CENT)

SERVES 2

350 g (¾ lb) potatoes, peeled and roughly chopped	2 cups peeled and roughly chopped potatoes
135 ml (4½ fl oz) skimmed milk	Generous ½ cup skim milk
2 x 120-g (4½-oz) pieces smoked cod	2 x 4½-oz pieces smoked cod
1 bay leaf	1 bay leaf
1 tsp cornflour	1 tsp cornstarch
1 tbsp water	1 tbsp water
Salt and freshly ground black pepper	Salt and freshly ground black pepper
2 carrots	2 carrots
90 g (3½ oz) broccoli	3½ oz calabrese
2 tbsp set plain yogurt or fromage frais	2 tbsp set plain yogurt or fromage blanc
2 meringue nests	2 meringue nests
60 g (2½ oz) blackberries	½ cup blackberries
Icing sugar, for dusting	Confectioners' sugar, for dusting

Pre-heat the oven to 170°C/325°F/gas 3.

Boil the potatoes until they are tender, then mash them, adding a little of the skimmed milk and season to taste.

Meanwhile, poach the pieces of cod in the remaining milk with the bay leaf for 10 minutes. Remove the fish to a warm plate and discard the bay leaf.

Mix the cornflour into a paste with the water. Pour this into the poaching liquid and stir over a medium heat until it thickens. Season to taste.

Flake the poached fish into an ovenproof dish and then pour the sauce over it. Top with the mashed potato and bake in the pre-heated oven for 20 minutes.

While the pie is baking, cook the carrots then lightly cook the broccoli in just a little water.

Once the pie is ready, place it under a hot grill for a few minutes to brown the top, then serve with the broccoli and carrots.

For dessert, place half the set yogurt or fromage frais in each of the meringue nests. Arrange the blackberries on top, sift a little icing sugar over the top and serve.

Cheats' Chicken Casserole with Mango and Ice-cream

PER SERVING: 404 CALORIES
9 G (¼ OZ) FAT (20 PER CENT)

SERVES 2

2 carrots, peeled and sliced	2 carrots, peeled and sliced
100 g (4 oz) mushrooms, wiped and chopped	2 cups wiped and chopped mushrooms
1 onion, peeled and sliced	1 onion, peeled and sliced
1 clove garlic, crushed	1 clove garlic, minced
150 g (5 oz) tinned chicken soup	Generous cup canned chicken soup
75 ml (3 fl oz) water	Scant ½ cup water
2 x 110-g (4-oz) lean chicken breasts	2 x 4-oz lean chicken breasts

Handful of fresh basil, chopped
Freshly ground black pepper
50 g (2 oz) sweetcorn
360 g (¾ lb) new potatoes, scrubbed
1 tsp chopped fresh mint, plus 2 sprigs to garnish
2 x 60-g (2½-oz) scoops ice-cream
4 slices fresh mango or other fruit of your choice

Handful of fresh basil, chopped
Freshly ground black pepper
½ cup sweetcorn
¾ lb new potatoes, scrubbed
1 tsp chopped fresh mint, plus 2 sprigs to garnish
2 x 2½-oz scoops ice-cream
4 slices fresh mango or other fruit of your choice

Pre-heat the oven to 180°C/350°F/gas 4.

Place the carrots, mushrooms, onion and garlic in a casserole dish with the soup and water and stir to mix. Add the chicken, basil and some freshly ground black pepper. Cover and bake in the pre-heated oven for 45 minutes.

Add the sweetcorn and cook for 15 more minutes.

Meanwhile, cook the potatoes with the mint, saving a few leaves to garnish, and serve with the casserole.

For dessert, serve a scoop of ice-cream with 2 slices of mango or other fruit each.

Fettucine with Prosciutto

PER SERVING: 407 CALORIES
10 G (¼ OZ) FAT (23 PER CENT)

SERVES 2

1 onion, sliced
2 tbsp olive oil
50 g (2 oz) prosciutto,
cut into strips
2 tbsp half-fat single cream
Freshly ground black pepper
150 g (5 oz) green fettucine
90 g (3½ oz) frozen peas
½ crisp lettuce
½ a green pepper, deseeded
and finely chopped

1 onion, sliced
2 tbsp olive oil
2 oz prosciutto, cut into strips
2 tbsp half-fat light cream
Freshly ground black pepper
5 oz green fettucine
Scant cup frozen peas
½ crisp lettuce
½ a green bell pepper, deseeded
and finely chopped

Cook the onion in the oil until it is soft. Add the prosciutto and the cream. Season to taste with pepper, cover and keep warm.

Cook the fettucine in plenty of boiling salted water. Once it is boiling, add the frozen peas and cook for 8 to 10 minutes. Drain and spoon half on to each plate. Pour the prosciutto and cream sauce over the pasta and serve with a green salad of lettuce and green pepper.

Steak and Chips with a Nectarine

PER SERVING: 393 CALORIES
11 G (¼ OZ) FAT (25 PER CENT)

SERVES 1

100 g (4 oz) lean steak	4 oz lean steak
1 large tomato, halved	1 large tomato, halved
1 large mushroom	1 large mushroom
100 g (4 oz) oven chips	4 oz oven chips
Ketchup (optional)	Catsup (optional)
1 large nectarine	1 large nectarine

Grill the steak, tomato halves and mushroom.

Meanwhile, cook the oven chips according to the instructions on the pack. Serve all together, with tomato ketchup if liked. Have the nectarine for dessert.

Salmon and Prawn Rice with Melon and Port

PER SERVING:

404 CALORIES

6 G (⅛ OZ) FAT (13 PER CENT)

SERVES 2

110 g (4 oz) brown rice	⅔ cup brown rice
50 g (2 oz) prawns	2 oz shrimp
Pinch of paprika	Pinch of paprika
2 tbsp sherry	2 tbsp sherry
75 g (3 oz) quark	Scant ½ cup ricotta
Freshly ground black pepper	Freshly ground black pepper
70 g (3 oz) tinned salmon, flaked	½ cup drained canned salmon, flaked
2 spring onions, chopped	2 scallions, chopped
½ galia melon	½ galia melon
1 tbsp port	1 tbsp port
2 sprigs of mint	2 sprigs of mint

Cook the rice according to the instructions on the pack.

Meanwhile, mix the prawns with the paprika, sherry, quark and season to taste with pepper. Heat the mixture in a pan until almost boiling, then stir in the salmon and heat for a further 8 minutes.

When the rice is cooked, mix in the spring onions, spoon it on to 2 plates and pour the salmon sauce over it.

For dessert, cut the melon away from its skin and slice. Pour the port over the melon and garnish each serving with a sprig of mint. Chill until ready to eat.

Indigestion Remedies Available from Pharmacies and Chemists

Product	Active ingredient
Powders	
BiSoDol Original	Magnesium carbonate, sodium bicarbonate
Eno Powder	Sodium bicarbonate, citric acid, sodium carbonate
Original Andrews Salts	Sodium bicarbonate, Magnesium sulphate
Liquids	
Boots Cream of Magnesia	Magnesium oxide, magnesium sulphate
Gaviscon Liquid	Sodium bicarbonate, aluminium hydroxide, calcium carbonate
Asilone Liquid	Aluminium hydroxide, simethicone/dimethicone, magnesium hydroxide
Asilone Suspension	Simethicone/dimethicone, aluminium hydroxide, magnesium hydroxide
Aludrox Liquid	Aluminium hydroxide
Milk of Magnesia	Magnesium hydroxide
Pepto-Bismol	Bismuth

Boots Double Action Indigestion Mixture	Aluminium hydroxide, magnesium hydroxide, simethicone/dimethicone

Tablets

Gaviscon 250	Alginic acid, sodium bicarbonate, aluminium hydroxide, magnesium trisilicate
Gaviscon 500 Extra Strength	Alginic acid, sodium bicarbonate, aluminium hydroxide, magnesium trisilicate
Milk of Magnesia Tablets	Magnesium hydroxide
Asilone Tablets	Simethicone/dimethicone, aluminium hydroxide
Andrews Antacid	Calcium carbonate, magnesium carbonate
Aludrox	Aluminium hydroxide, magnesium carbonate, magnesium hydroxide
Setlers	Calcium carbonate
Setlers Tums	Calcium carbonate
Remegel	Calcium carbonate
Rennie	Calcium carbonate, magnesium carbonate
Rennie Rap-Eze	Calcium carbonate
Rennie Gold	Calcium carbonate
BiSoDol Original	Calcium carbonate, magnesium carbonate, sodium bicarbonate
BiSoDol Extra	Calcium carbonate, magnesium carbonate, sodium bicarbonate, simethicone
BiSoDol Heartburn	Magaldrate, alginic acid, sodium bicarbonate

Boots Double Action Indigestion Tablets	Alginic acid, magnesium hydroxide
Lloyds Antacid Tablets	Calcium carbonate
Superdrug Indigestion Tablets	Calcium carbonate, magnesium carbonate

Other products

Zantac 75	Ranitidine
Tagamet 100	Cimetidine
Pepcid AC	Famotidine

Index

Meal suggestions are listed in chapter 7. Only the recipes have been indexed, but if, for example, a breakfast is wanted, the inclusive page references are at 'breakfasts'.

Of further interest . . .

Healing Through Nutrition

*A natural approach to treating 50
common illnesses with diet and nutrients*

Dr Melvyn R. Werbach

This indispensable reference book provides the nutritional roots of and treatments for 50 common illnesses, from allergies and the common cold to cancer.

The world's authority on the relationship between nutrition and illness, Dr Melvyn Werbach makes it easy to learn what you can do to influence the course of your health via the nutrients that you feed your body.

A chapter is devoted to each of the 50 ailments and this highly accessible A-Z of nutritional health includes:

- an analysis of dietary factors affecting health and well-being
- a suggested healing diet for 50 common illnesses
- nutritional healing plans, with recommended dosages for vitamins, minerals and other essential nutrients
- an explanation of vitamin supplements and how they can improve your health

There are also guidelines on how to plan the right healing diet for yourself and how to diagnose food sensitivities. With this groundbreaking guide you will be able to make informed decisions about the essential role of nutrients in your health and well-being.

Recipes for Health:
Irritable Bowel Syndrome

Jill Davies and Ann Page Wood

Irritable Bowel Syndrome, or IBS, is a very common bowel disorder which accounts for over 50 per cent of referrals to gastro-intestinal clinics. What you eat is of great importance in helping to control this condition.

Specialists usually advise a high-fibre diet – and many sufferers benefit from a diet low in fat and high in protein.

This practical guide can be used in conjunction with your doctor's treatment. The authors:

- explain what is meant by the term 'irritable bowel syndrome'
- discuss the various physical and psychological factors associated with the disorder
- give guidelines on coping with IBS

The tempting recipes are based on cereals, fruit and vegetables, and high-protein foods. The amount of fibre is given in each dish.

With this book, you can help yourself to better health and learn to cope with and even overcome your IBS.

Stress

Proven stress-coping strategies for better health

Leon Chaitow

Do you suffer from migraine, chronic back pain, frequent colds, fatigue, panic attacks or high blood pressure? If so, you could be suffering from stress which can damage your health.

Stress has a disastrous effect on our immune systems, and can be the major cause of both mild and serious health problems. Psychoneuroimmunology, or PNI, is the science which holds the key to many common health problems. It points to new ways in which damaging emotions can be controlled, so protecting our bodies' natural defences and warding off illness.

Leading health writer, Leon Chaitow, uses the latest research into the mind/body connection to help you create your own stress protection plan. Advice on diet, exercise, meditation, relaxation, guided imagery and visualization, with useful checklists, will help you develop your own system to cope with the inevitable pressures of everyday life.

The Book of Pain Relief

Leon Chaitow

Pain is the body's warning signal, a vital protective mechanism which alerts us that something is wrong. Chronic pain, however, serves no useful purpose and can trigger other physical and emotional problems, while long-term use of medication can make the underlying problem worse. Health expert Leon Chaitow explains how to break the never-ending cycle of pain, medication and misery, so that pain is eased or even removed altogether.

This definitive guide to how pain may affect any part of the body allows you to discover what's right for you; many beneficial treatments can be carried out at home, and the practical solutions include:

- self-help methods for immediate relief
- how to release the body's own natural pain-killers
- how dietary changes can help
- acupuncture, electrotherapy and massage
- herbal remedies, homoeopathy and aromatherapy
- the benefits of water treatment
- healing and therapeutic touch
- the role of relaxation and stress reduction

This is an empowering book that will help us regain control of our bodies and our lives.

Let's Eat Right to Keep Fit

Adelle Davis

Here Adelle Davis presents information concerning our bodies' vital nutritional processes which is both authoritative and fascinating. Her recommendations for a balanced diet are important for anyone interested in preventive medicine.

Over 40 nutrients needed by the body for health are discussed in detail and the foods that supply them are listed.

Described by *Time* magazine as 'the highest authority in the kitchen', the value of good wholesome food over synthetic foods is stressed throughout. This book remains a bible for anyone interested in health or food – from doctors to cooks.

Let's Get Well

Adelle Davis

Let's Get Well explains how a well chosen diet, which provides the most needed nutrients, can repair and rebuild a sick body. Packed full of information on every aspect of health and nutrition, it is an ideal reference book for the way we live today.

Adelle Davis explains the function of nutrition in diseases related to the blood system, the digestion, the liver, the kidneys and the nervous system. Illnesses covered include heart attacks, ulcers, diabetes, arthritis, gout and anaemia. Her clear explanations, with full medical references, will guide the way to better health.

Healthy by Nature

Beth MacEoin

How can women keep a healthy balance in their lives today? With so many demands being placed on women as homemakers, business women, mothers and carers, how can we make sure we take care of ourselves? *Healthy by Nature* shows how even the busiest schedule can make room for healthy improvements. Well-known homoeopath Beth MacEoin shows how to break the downward spiral of overwork, tiredness and anxiety and enjoy new vitality and enthusiasm for life – without having to follow a harsh regime.

Describing how to set realistic goals, she reveals the benefits of homoeopathy and shows how acupuncture, herbalism, hypnotherapy, osteopathy, massage and aromatherapy can help, giving sensible guidelines that take the practicalities of busy lives into account. For physical, emotional and mental well-being, *Healthy by Nature* is the essential guide to living in harmony with your body.

HEALING THROUGH NUTRITION	0 7225 2941 4	£16.99	☐
RECIPES FOR HEALTH: IBS	0 7225 3141 9	£5.99	☐
STRESS	0 7225 3192 3	£5.99	☐
BOOK OF PAIN RELIEF	0 7225 2820 5	£7.99	☐
LET'S EAT RIGHT TO KEEP FIT	0 7225 3203 2	£5.99	☐
LET'S GET WELL	0 7225 2701 2	£5.99	☐
HEALTHY BY NATURE	0 7225 2803 5	£9.99	☐

All these books are available from your local bookseller or can be ordered direct from the publishers.

To order direct just tick the titles you want and fill in the form below:

Name: _____

Address: _____

_____

_____ Postcode _____

Send to Thorsons Mail Order, Dept 3, HarperCollins *Publishers*, Westerhill Road, Bishopbriggs, Glasgow G64 2QT.

Please enclose a cheque or postal order or your authority to debit your Visa/Access account —

Credit card no: _____

Expiry date: _____

Signature: _____

— up to the value of the cover price plus:

UK & BFPO: Add £1.00 for the first book and 25p for each additional book ordered.

Overseas orders including Eire: Please add £2.95 service charge. Books will be sent by surface mail but quotes for airmail dispatches will be given on request.

24-HOUR TELEPHONE ORDERING SERVICE FOR ACCESS/VISA CARDHOLDERS — TEL: 0141 772 2281.